MW00629035

Trusting
GOD
in Trying Times

Trusting
GOD
in Trying Times

STUDIES in THE BOOK of HABAKKUK

———————— Don Green ————————

Trusting God in Trying Times is the kind of book I imagine no one wants to have to write. The obvious reason for this is because if it's going to have any real impact, depth, or sincerity, the author has likely had to hold God's hand through some incredibly difficult and dark times of his own (something no one would envy). Yet, as Spurgeon once said, "I have looked back to times of trial with a kind of longing, not to have them return, but to feel the strength of God as I have felt it then." This book embodies that ethos. Sadly, a number of other works on this subject matter are either theologically inaccurate, doctrinally superficial, or patronizingly self-oriented, lacking the elixir of God's Word. On the other hand, what Don Green has done in this book is what I've always known him to do as a preacher: perfectly wed doctrinal accuracy with soul-piercing application in a way I've never seen from any other man alive. He embodies the pastoral and heavenly precision of the Puritans in a devotional way, but without the verbosity. Regardless of the reader's own situation, this book is a must-read for anyone wanting to prepare for difficult times—or minister to others currently facing them.

PETER SAMMONS, PhD: Assistant Professor in Theology, The Master's Seminary, Sun Valley, CA; Author of: *Reprobation and the Sovereignty of God* (Kregel Academic: 2022)

Imagine that you could sit down with a seasoned, gracious pastor, and that you were encouraged to lay out to him your woes and heartaches. Imagine then that he took the time to pour out for you, as it were, a glass brimming with scriptural truth, such as would ease your pains and lift your spirit. That is what you will find in this book. Don Green has produced a work of encouragement, which will surely "strengthen the hands that are weak and the knees that are feeble" (Heb. 12:12) among weary and bruised believers. Don takes us through the book of Habakkuk in an approach that is equally expository and pastoral. The spirit of his writing hails not from an ivory tower, but from a life lived in the trenches with the rest of us. In reading some pastor-authors, I mentally prefix the word "theoretically" to much of their work. I never did that with Don's writing. You will benefit richly from it, and you will want to give copies to your friends.

DAN PHILLIPS: Pastor, Copperfield Bible Church, Houston, TX; Author of *The World-Tilting Gospel* (Kregel: 2011), and *God's Wisdom in Proverbs* (Kress: 2011)

It is a pleasure for me to recommend Don Green's book, *Trusting God in Trying Times*. Writing as a skilled expositor and compassionate pastor, Don unfolds the book of Habakkuk. With great transparency of his own soul Don communicates the message of this Old Testament prophet while urging us to apply its truths to our lives. If you are looking for a book to encourage your heart by helping you to trust God in the difficulties of life, then you will want to read *Trusting God in Trying Times*. It ministered greatly to me, and I am confident it will do the same for you.

STEVE KRELOFF: Pastor/Teacher, Lakeside Community Chapel, Clearwater, FL

Has the giant named Fear caused you to languish away in the valley of trouble and affliction? God would not have you to lie there in defeat, but would rather take you up into the delectable mountains of spiritual peace and joy in Him. In this book you have a trustworthy map to take you there; and in Pastor Don, a faithful shepherd to show you the way.

KYLE REEDER: Pastor, Solid Rock Baptist Church, Benton, KY

A. W. Tozer famously said, "It is doubtful whether God can bless a man greatly until he has hurt him deeply." Pain, of course, does not automatically lead to blessing, but it does always provide an opportunity to think deeply the meaning and purpose of life. It had that impact on Don Green as a newlywed lawyer. The years-long struggle took him on a journey of learning what it means to trust God in trying times. Through honest dealings with his own soul and humble study of the Word of God, he gained insights that he has generously and pastorally passed along in this book. By tracing God's dealings with the Old Testament prophet, Habakkuk, Green carefully charts the path from heartache to joy that is available to every follower of Christ. Seeing that path, and staying on it, is the great lesson of *Trusting God in Trying Times*. I am saddened by the deep hurt that Don Green suffered as a young man, but I praise God for the deep blessings that have resulted in his life as a faithful pastor and teacher of Scripture. In this wonderful book, those blessings overflow in encouragement and comfort for all who will read it and take its counsel to heart.

TOM ASCOL: Pastor, Grace Baptist Church of Cape Coral, FL; President of Founders Ministries and The Institute of Public Theology

Adversity and affliction, suffering and sorrow, pain and perplexity—these are tools in the skillful, omnipotent hand of a loving Father who is good and wise. God's intent is to train His elect, to disciple His people, so that no matter the difficulty, no matter the circumstance, they will anchor their confidence in His perfect Word, set their hope fully on Him, and settle their hearts in the peace that passes all understanding. God is their refuge, the place of perfect rest for their weary souls. This is the thesis Don Green pursues with theological precision and pastoral warmth. He clearly respects his readers, writing in plain and simple language—like an older brother in the faith who has walked with God, proven His truths, and found Him trustworthy—he calls his readers to follow him to the safe harbor of trust in God. The result of this labor of love is an accessible book, full of pastoral wisdom. The reward for the reader is the real-life, time-tested comfort Don has received from Christ and a plan, for any who struggle, of how to trust God in trying times.

TRAVIS ALLEN: Pastor, Grace Church of Greeley, Greeley, CO

Trusting God in Trying Times
Studies in the Book of Habakkuk

Don Green

ISBN: 978–0–9987156–1–2

Cover design and typeset by www.greatwriting.org

Printed in the United States of America

Trust the Word Press
575 Chamber Drive
Milford, OH 45150

TRUST THE WORD
PRESS
BIBLICAL THINKING FOR BIBLICAL LIVING

To the memory of

Gilbert Ray Green

the earthly father whom my heavenly Father wisely and lovingly appointed as an instrument to draw me closer to Himself.

Acknowledgments

Many people have made this book possible. It's a daunting task to thank some for fear of omitting others. God has blessed me with the support of family and friends in ministry without whom you would not have this book to read.

Jim Holmes patiently guided me through the editorial process and applied his creative gifts to the cover design and print layout. Carl Dobrowolski worked behind the scenes to introduce it into the stream of commerce. I'm grateful to them both for their experience and friendship.

Gary Nelson is a skilled attorney who has advised me on intellectual property rights for over twenty years, including my venture into publishing. (He is also the only person I know to summit Mount Everest.) My professional respect and appreciation for him knows no bounds.

Several friends reviewed the manuscript and made constructive comments. Their input made this book better than it would have been. I'm grateful for Travis Allen, Tom Ascol, Garry Knussman, Steve Kreloff, Dan Phillips, Kyle Reeder, and Peter Sammons.

Only God knows the contribution of Peter and Barb Coeler to my life and family. Over a decade ago, they gave me the use of their remote cabin for several days to do my earliest work on this book. They are exemplary Christians who have blessed so many with their love.

In a prior generation, Martyn Lloyd-Jones wrote a small book titled *From Fear to Faith*. Every page of this book is soaked with its influence.

I am especially grateful to John MacArthur for reading the manuscript and writing such a gracious foreword to commend the book to you. He is a wise leader and a kind friend. My pulpit bears the indelible imprint of his ministry. My earlier book, *John MacArthur: An Insider's Tribute*, is a better expression of my appreciation than anything I could say here.

My mother, Geraldine Green, has trusted God through many trying times in her eighty-nine years. She is a quietly remarkable and resilient woman who first laid the foundation of Christian truth in my heart. It is such a blessing that she is still with us.

My children have stood beside me faithfully through years of seminary training and ministry life. They are all a gift from the Lord: Hannah, Gretchen, Daniel (and his lovely wife, Lindsey), Julie, Addie, and Marisa.

My earnest prayer is for the salvation of my grandchildren and that one day this book will minister to them as well. God knows how precious Gabrielle, Everett, and Alexandria are to my heart.

But none of my adult life or ministry would have been possible without the love and support of Nancy. She walked with me through the trying times that this book describes. She is a noble Christian woman and a faithful wife. She also read the manuscript and made important contributions to its final form.

Yet all those horizontal acknowledgements yield to this vertical acknowledgement: God has been gracious in Christ to this unworthy sinner.

Soli Deo Gloria.

Foreword

John MacArthur
. . . .

Scripture tells us that "the sufferings of this present time are not worthy to be compared with the glory that is to be revealed" (Rom. 8:18). That's a welcome and reassuring maxim, but most of us at one point or another will have an experience of profound adversity, heartbreak, catastrophe, or other form of suffering that will test our belief in that promise. Perhaps you have experienced such a trial, and it felt like an unending ordeal that might tear you away from any spiritual mooring.

For Don Green it was the untimely death of his father and brother—a bitter, unexpected loss that left him gasping for relief in a sea of dark grief and spiritual upheaval. At the time, Don was a young believer with a fresh understanding of the gospel, full of joy and anticipating an abundant life. But then this unthinkably severe family tragedy suddenly overwhelmed him with sorrow and raised questions he had no answers for.

Why do faithful people suffer, especially while evildoers seem to prosper? How can a believer lay hold of the biblical promises about blessedness and well-being when shackled to a load of anguish? Why does God sometimes seem silent (or absent altogether) when we call out to Him for relief? And why does He seem to delay His help when we feel we are at the very end of our endurance? Why me? Why this? Why now? "Why do You stand afar off, O LORD? Why do You hide Yourself in times of trouble?" (Ps. 10:1). "O LORD, why do You reject my soul? Why do You hide Your face from me?" (Ps. 88:14).

Those are common questions, asked and mulled over by

good and godly people throughout human history. Even Jesus cried out on the cross, "My God, My God, why have You forsaken Me?" (Matt. 27:46).

There are answers to those questions. Not necessarily complete explanations, but biblical promises and encouragements enough to carry us through to safety.

Don Green found answers in an unexpected place: the ancient writings of the Old Testament prophet Habakkuk. In the volume you are holding, he poignantly describes his own journey through that terrible trial, and then he gives a clear and perceptive analysis of Habakkuk's dialogue with Yahweh on the subject of human suffering.

No matter who you are or where you are in life, I know you will benefit greatly from Pastor Green's insights on the prophecy of Habakkuk and the problem of human misery. A careful study of these truths will prepare you for trials that may yet lie in your future, and it can also help lead you out of that dark dungeon of sorrow that this world's troubles so often try to confine us in.

Habakkuk reminds us that Yahweh is the God of our salvation, He is our strength, and He will bring us through whatever storm the troubles of this life take us into. This is an exhilarating study, from a man who knows what it is to weather that storm.

The Pastor Who Missed the Point

When Good Men Misread Broken Hearts
. . . .

Then Job answered, "I have heard many such things;
sorry comforters are you all."
(Job 16:1–2)

I was a young Christian, sitting with a pastor renowned for his understanding of spiritual life.

"This is it," I thought. "*Finally* I have someone who can help me overcome my discouragement." I poured my heart out to him, describing the heavy clouds that hung over my soul. Now I waited to hear the words that would unlock my return to intimacy with God.

Sadly, my anticipation would have no reward. He quickly showed that he had no idea how to help me. His deep reservoir of spiritual experience prompted him to say, "You need to trust God. That is the answer. Isn't it?"

I sat quietly and looked at him without saying a word.

He raised his voice: "*Isn't it?*"

As if increased volume could solve my spiritual problems.

I suppressed my desire to mock him—slapping myself on the forehead and saying, "Oh, of course! Trust God! Why didn't *I* think of that?"

Despite his reputation and his good intentions, the pastor had completely missed the point. He made the common mistake of turning an important biblical command into an empty platitude that carried no power of persuasion to my troubled heart. He was not wrong . . . but he was not helpful.

I already knew I was *supposed* to trust God. I *wanted* to trust God. But life was crushing me, and I didn't know where to turn. Yelling at me to trust God didn't advance the discussion at all. And so I walked away from him more discouraged than before.

That pastor didn't understand the question that was really on the table: *How* do I trust God? How can I have confidence in Him when life seems to collapse all around me? How can I depend on Him when circumstances are spinning out of control?

The answer to that "how" question matters to every true Christian. That answer will transform your life and lighten the load of your troubled heart—no matter *what* your struggles may be. It will lead you to joy even if your circumstances cannot change. Best of all, it is available for every believer in Jesus Christ.

In other words, beloved Christian, the answer is for *you*. God's Word assures you there is a path to joy inexpressible and full of glory, even in the face of trials that have discouraged you for a very long time (1 Peter 1:6–9).

Even if you are not a Christian, I invite you to examine these pages with an open Bible and an open heart. Ultimately, your answer is found in the Lord Jesus Christ. I wrote Chapter 14 especially for you. May God turn your earthly sorrow to eternal joy.

One final word: I'm especially sympathetic to the discouraged reader who may be jaded after counselors, pastors, books, or well-intentioned friends failed to provide any meaningful encouragement. How many miles I've walked in your shoes!

I've included a measure of personal testimony here, not because my life story is intrinsically important, but to assure you that I do not speak from the theologian's ivory tower. No, I speak as an eyewitness to living, biblical realities that delivered me from an abominable black dungeon of despair. My testimony is only a window to the real substance of this book— the true knowledge of a great God and Savior who can be trusted in *all* His dealings with His children. I want the comfort Christ showered on me to become yours in exceedingly abundant measure (2 Cor. 1:3–4). I am on your side.

May God use this book greatly to His glory.

1

I Didn't See This Coming

Who Knows What Tomorrow Will Bring?

• •

*Yet you do not know what your life will be like tomorrow. You are
just a vapor that appears for a little while and then vanishes away.
(James 4:14)*

My Life Before Christ

The truth claims of the biblical gospel set the context for the discouragement I shared with that pastor.

The Bible tells us that all people have sinned and fallen short of the glory of God (Rom. 3:23). As a result, we all are spiritually dead, under the wrath of God, and subject to eternal punishment (Eph. 2:1–3).

The only solution to that dilemma is found in Jesus Christ. The eternal Son of God took on human flesh, lived a perfect life, and then offered Himself as a sacrifice to God to pay for the sins of everyone who would ever believe in Him (2 Cor. 5:21). Only those who repent of their sins and believe in Christ will be saved (John 14:6; Acts 4:12). God will judge all others and consign them to eternal hell as the just punishment for their rebellion against Him (Rev. 20:11–15).

True Christians understand that. They look with mercy on unbelievers and long for them to come to know Christ. The thought of a loved one suffering eternal punishment motivates a Christian to prayer and evangelism (*cf.* Rom. 10:1, 14–17).

So it was with me and my dad.

I grew up as a non-Christian in the shadow of a spiritually indifferent father. My mom took me to Sunday School at a country church, but throughout my childhood years I never put my faith in Christ. Mom tried to bring a biblical dynamic to our family life, but with Dad around, she didn't have much to work with—and *I* certainly didn't help the situation!

Both Mom and Dad grew up in rural, southern Indiana in comparative poverty. Dad was an intelligent but uneducated man. He quit school after the eighth grade, content to earn his living by working with his hands—first as a car mechanic and much later as an airplane mechanic.

He was respected in the community. He was once a candidate for county sheriff. He raised funds to improve the city park. He generously provided free plane rides to anyone who asked.

It was different in our home. We knew Dad as a severe man. He was the guy who, with his bare hands, disarmed a would-be assailant who pulled a gun on him at close range. He wasn't content *just* to take the gun away, however. As the foiled attacker watched in astonishment, Dad threw his gun on the ground repeatedly until it shattered into pieces. The attacker learned an important lesson.

You don't mess with Gilbert.

Dad also had a unique response when he was the "victim" of road rage. We were driving on a family vacation in the early 1970s when Dad pulled onto an interstate. For reasons I will never understand, a car approached us rapidly from behind and swerved to within three feet of us at sixty miles per hour while some wild-eyed woman hung out of the passenger window yelling obscenities at Dad.

Bad move.

While my astonished jaw dropped to the floor in the back seat, Dad struck back. He accelerated and actually swerved *closer* to the attacking vehicle. He stuck his left arm out the window and tried desperately to pound his fist on the hood of their car—all the while delivering a few expletives from his *own* vocabulary. We were *inches* away from what could have been a multiple-fatality collision.

Not surprisingly, the other driver reconsidered the importance of the fight. In response to my dad's apparent lunacy, he slowed down to about thirty miles per hour until we had pulled away and were safely out of sight. He had gotten the point.

You don't mess with Gilbert.

Unfortunately, the harshness that gave rise to those colorful stories played out in our home life in less entertaining ways. Sadly, Dad was often a coarse, selfish man who ruled our home by intimidation. He cursed. He pounded tables. He routinely stayed home watching TV while I went off to my Little League baseball games. He withheld his mechanical skills when I had bicycle problems I didn't know how to fix.

Years later, I now realize it could have been worse. But to my shame, I had no affection for him when I left home to attend Indiana University (IU). It was far from my only shame.

My Conversion

Somewhere in the midst of my high school years, a well-intentioned young woman shared her faith with me (a faith that was not the true gospel). It sounded too good to be true. If I simply believed that Jesus Christ was the Son of God, I could be a Christian. How simple! I affirmed my belief in that minimalistic creed, and she responded by welcoming me into the kingdom of God. I mistakenly claimed to be a Christian on that flimsy basis for several years.

Any objective look at my life would have exposed the lie. I did not love Jesus Christ (1 Cor. 16:22). I never read the Bible in a meaningful way (John 8:31–32). I did not fellowship with Christians in a Bible-believing church (Heb. 10:24–25). Internally, I was an angry, carnal man, even if I usually hid it from those around me (Gal. 5:19–21). I called Jesus "Lord" but lived in total disregard to Him (Matt. 7:21–23). In short, I was dead in my sins, dominated by the devil, and doomed to suffer the wrath of God (Eph. 2:1–3).

I hid my spiritual shame with a reasonable work ethic and a good academic career during my undergraduate days at IU. I studied political science and criminal justice—interests that eventually led me to IU's law school. I had no interest in "justice"—I just coveted the wealth and prestige I thought a legal career could bring.

But God had different plans for my life.

The seeds of change were sown in my daily routine at the law library. In a habit positively bizarre for an aspiring lawyer, I started each day by reading a newspaper column written by a well-known Christian evangelist. Usually, he had simple advice for people with counseling questions: Repent of your sins and trust Christ as your Lord and Savior. I read that column faithfully for months, even though I would have scoffed at the notion that *I* needed his advice. After all, I thought I *was* a Christian.

In other words, I never saw Christ coming.

And I *sure* didn't see Him coming when I started partying with a friend on a cold November night in 1983. We were having a great time, when, in the midst of the revelry, I thought to myself, "I'm sinning against God. But I don't care. I'm going to do what *I* want to do." So I drank my fill of sin late into the night.

The next morning, I looked bleary-eyed into my bathroom mirror and a wicked grin curled across my lips. "You really tied one on last night," I told myself. I was proud of my sin.

In the very next moment, sheer terror pierced my heart. *"You call yourself a Christian? How could you do the things you did last night?"* In that eternally momentous instant, my spiritual world collapsed. I knew I was a fraud. I was so ashamed. I deserved the full wrath of God for my sin.

The fear of God overwhelmed my soul. Sixty seconds after I had boasted over my sin, I was convinced of this terrifying thought: "If I don't receive Christ *right now*, I will go to hell forever." I needed to repent of my sins and receive Christ as my Lord and Savior—just as that newspaper column had been telling me for months.

I rushed into my bedroom and knelt beside my bed. I prayed something like, "Lord Jesus, I've always thought that I was a Christian, but now I'm not sure. I know I'm a sinner. I believe You died to save me from my sins. Lord Jesus, I *really and truly* want to receive You as my Lord and Savior. Come into my life and save me."

There was no magic to the precise words of the prayer. The repentant reality God wrought in my heart is what mattered. And at that moment—which God had ordained before the foundation of the world—Jesus Christ saved this sinner who called on His name (Eph. 1:4; Rom. 10:13).

Christ and a New Love for Dad

The change Christ made in my life was immediate and dramatic. Without any external prompting, I started reading my Bible. It thrilled my heart. I could understand what I was reading and the thought, "This is true! This is true!" reverberated throughout my mind. I knew joy, peace, and a spiritual transformation that only comes when God makes someone a new creature in Christ (2 Cor. 5:17).

Before long, my new life in Christ had an impact on my relationship with my dad. The starting point was my own attitude. Whatever his failings were, he was entitled to my honor and respect (Ex. 20:12). But beyond that, I saw him as a lost soul in danger of eternal judgment in hell. My heart was greatly burdened for his salvation, so I started praying for him daily. I wanted him to know Christ and the forgiveness of his sins.

Only one problem. When it came to spiritual things . . .

You didn't mess with Gilbert.

Dad was hostile toward my conversion in the early months of my Christian life. One evening, he started a particularly uncomfortable conversation. Drawing upon his tried-and-true intimidation methods, he sat me down in the living room to give me a good talking-to about "religion."

I think he instinctively knew he was out of his element, because he was visibly uncomfortable. He shifted around on the couch and eventually put his iron fist in a velvet glove. "I've always been real proud of you," he started. "When you do something, you put everything you have into it. And . . . and"—he struggled with the transition—"I'm glad you're real religious and all. But you've taken it too far. And I want it to stop."

He paused for my reaction, surely expecting the same

capitulation he had seen from that assailant years ago, from the driver on the interstate, from virtually everyone who had ever heard him bark a command in their direction.

But not this time. God had brought a defining moment to my life.

Intimidate my *soul*? Intimidate my *conscience*? Deny the Lord Jesus Christ who had saved me from my sins and imparted a new life, filled with immeasurable gladness, that culminates in heaven? No. Absolutely not. Not in this life; not in a thousand lifetimes.

"No, Dad. Jesus Christ has changed my life. I'll never stop following Him."

I had just messed with Gilbert.

My answer left him speechless. He left the room, and I didn't see him for the rest of the evening. I went back to my bedroom to read my Bible, blissfully unaware that I had created a rift in which he would become even more hostile and distant to me than before.

Thankfully, by the power of Christ, Dad's hostility made me love him all the more. I deepened my commitment to pray for him, prove myself a faithful son, and trust God to work in his heart over time. If my lips weren't persuasive, perhaps my life would be.

The years went by, and I made a special effort to reach out to Dad. We lived about five hours apart, so I called him often and went to visit when I could. I began talking to him about my work and personal life. To my surprise, he quickly became a trusted confidant. He took great interest in my legal career, and our relationship warmed even further when I brought Nancy home to announce our engagement. I think Dad looked at Nancy and saw I had some sense after all!

Behind the scenes, our improved relationship fueled my daily prayers for Dad's salvation. "God, save my dad. I don't care if You do anything else, my Father, just save my dad. *Even if it takes a tragedy*, please bring my dad to salvation." I was trusting God for that. My private prayers deepened as our personal bond grew closer.

Undoubtedly, the highlight was Labor Day weekend, 1988. We went to breakfast and talked about his past. We walked downtown and crawled under a train locomotive so Dad could explain to me how it worked. We sat outside on lawn chairs and discussed the nature of Christianity.

My "strategy" was a budding success. God was obviously working in Dad's heart. I could *taste* the day when he would receive Christ. I was rejoicing in the obvious goodness of God.

When it came time to leave at the end of the weekend, the goodbye was especially sweet. We had enjoyed a great time together. I could have hugged him, but when it came to physical affection . . .

You didn't mess with Gilbert.

So I simply shook his hand and squeezed it firmly. I spent an extra moment looking in his face. I see it to this day. I genuinely loved him.

"See you later," I said.

"See you later," he replied.

I didn't see it coming.

We were wrong.

I never saw him again.

Gilbert Green, standing on Runway 5 at the North Vernon, Indiana airport in February 1988. Nine months later, wearing the same hat, he would perish in the trees seen in the distant background over his right shoulder.
Photo by *The Columbus Republic*. All rights reserved.

2

This Is Where It Ends?

The News You Never Want to Hear
. . . .

*My tears have been my food day and night, while they say to me
all day long, "Where is your God?"*
(Psalm 42:3)

Nancy and I had been married four months. We were enjoying our first Thanksgiving with guests with plans to see my parents the next day.

The call came in the middle of dinner.

"Your dad and your brother are dead."

I was stunned.

"There was a plane crash. You need to get home right away."

Eventually I pieced together that my dad and brother had taken a quick spin in Dad's new single-engine plane after finishing their Thanksgiving dinner. Dad was an experienced pilot, but for some reason on that clear November day, his plane crashed in a wooded area about a mile from the runway. He was sixty. My brother was thirty-six.[1]

Nancy threw some clothes into a suitcase, and we drove to be with my mom and to make funeral arrangements. When we arrived, the television crews had come and gone. Soon I was in the living room, watching news reports that carried interviews with family friends and video footage from the crash site. *"Gilbert Green and his son Roger were killed today in a single-engine plane crash near the North Vernon airport."* I sat slumped on the couch and shook my head at what I was seeing. It was *un*believable.

The next day, the coroner took me to the crash site. He had been among the first responders on the scene and officially

---

1 The dual loss of my brother, Roger, was a separate shock all its own. It's no dishonor to his memory that I do not discuss him or his family (whom I love) in this book; space constraints simply did not allow me the opportunity.

pronounced that Dad and Roger were dead. He filled me in on some details as we drove to the wooded area where the plane had gone down.

When we arrived, we found that the state police had sealed off the crash site to preserve it intact until federal investigators could arrive. The coroner intervened with the state trooper and secured permission for us to go closer to the plane.

We shuffled through the fallen autumn leaves toward the plane, which was about fifty yards away. I reached the yellow police tape and took in everything I possibly could. Nearly thirty-five years later, I still see it all with the same vividness. The broken plane. The twisted propeller. My brother's bloody jacket. My dad's favorite hat sitting upside down on the left wing. The broken tree branches, up and to my right, giving silent testimony to the angle of descent.

I stood behind the yellow tape and stared. The broken, 1971 orange-and-white Gulfstream (Grumman) AA1A, a two-seat plane bearing registration number N9396L, silently taunted my years of spiritual earnestness.

I shook my head. This was *un*believable. I asked under my breath, "*So this is where it ends? So this is where it ends?*" A torrent of questions rained down on my heart.

How could my dad—an experienced pilot—crash the plane in good weather a mile from the runway? You mean, I don't even get to say goodbye? Were their final moments filled with terror? My relationship with Dad is really over?

But the surpassing question that burdened my heart was this: *My years of praying for my dad's salvation end in a forsaken clump of trees in southern Indiana with no evidence that he trusted Christ?*

Forget the earthly consequences. My dad was dead—apparently without Christ and the forgiveness of his sins.

I had not been trusting God for *this*.

Imaginary voices mocked me mercilessly: "Where is your God?"

I turned and walked away.

I had no answer.

The North Vernon Sun

VOLUME 112—NO. 48 COPYRIGHT 1988 NORTH VERNON, INDIANA ★★ TUESDAY—NOVEMBER 29, 1988

The downed plane the day after the fatal crash—Staff photo by Phil Milholland

Gilbert Green, son, Roger die in plane crash Thursday

Gilbert Green, 60, manager of the North Vernon Municipal Airport and a veteran pilot and aircraft mechanic, and his son, Roger Green, 36, North Vernon, died instantly Thanksgiving Day when the two-seater plane they were in crashed, around 1:47 p.m., into a woods north of the field.

Deputy Jennings County coroner Gene Rudicel pronounced both men dead at the scene of the tragedy. He said the deaths were entirely due to injuries the pair suffered in the crash.

And that was the cause of death given by Dr. George Weir, pathologist at the hospital in Seymour, who performed the autopsies.

The plane was a two-seat, single engine 1970 Grumman Tiger AAI craft, which the older Green had just recently purchased. He owned two other planes, and planned to sell this one. Reportedly, he had only been up once in this plane prior to the fatal crash.

Thursday, at his residence at the airport, he talked to his son about his new acquisition, and said he wanted to show it to him. "You might even want to fly in this one," he added.

There were no eyewitnesses to the accident and it's not quite clear how long the plane had been aloft before it crashed.

But there were reports of people who did hear the plane's motor sputtering.

Gilbert Green was a most able pilot, and speculation among those who knew of his flying abilities what that whatever happened, it happened fast, or Green would have been able to maneuver the craft to nearby fields, instead of its plummeting into the woods.

The doomed plane hit a large stump in the woods with great force. However, the craft itself was not demolished, leading one person at the accident scene to speculate that the plane was only about 500 feet in the air when the trouble developed and it went down sharply.

Rescue 20, called to the scene, had to use its special equipment to extract the two bodies from the plane.

FFA officials from the district office in Indianapolis started an investigation of the crash Thanksgiving afternoon, sealing off the area where the plane went down for a time from news and TV photographers, and the general public. Reportedly, by the end of the week, they had taken the engine from the plane to their facilities for further study.

There was no fire due to the crash, but the North Vernon-Center Township Fire Department was called to the scene.

And the weather was exceptionally clear that day, with

extended visibility.

There never has been a fatal crash at the local field since it went into the city's hands. In fact, there has not even been any injuries suffered by anyone there in a plane accident.

However, in World War II, when the field was an auxiliary airport for Freeman Field in Seymour, an aviation cadet was killed in an accident there.

Gilbert took up flying back in 1965. That step sparked a deep and zealous interest that he never lost in both the local field and aircraft mechanics.

For 15 years, prior to taking over as manager of the field two years ago, he was an active member of the North Vernon Aviation Board and served a number of years in the key position of board president.

As such, he played a critical role in the many and extensive developments made at the local airport the past 17 years. According to fellow board mem-

bers, he was almost "Mr. Airport" in the loving attention he paid the facility and improvements there.

Glen Perkins, now president of the aviation board, said that he's been associated for all the past 17 years with Gilbert in the operation of the field. "The two of us never had a policy disagreement," Perkins noted. "He gave the airport everything he had."

Perkins also lauded Gilbert's abilities as a mechanic, saying he was very strict and a craftsman." He not only serviced private planes housed at the local field, but also had the same task for the Salem airport, and did service work for plane owners in Madison and Columbus.

His son, Roger, was a service manager of Seymour Auto Supply, a post he has held for the past three years. Prior to that he was employed by Carpenter Body Works in North Vernon, Connaughton Chevrolet and Horst

(Continued on Page 2)

Gilbert Green

Roger Green

The North Vernon Sun from November 29, 1988, tells the story.

National Transportation Safety Board

FACTUAL REPORT
AVIATION

NTSB Accident/Incident Number

C|H|5|8|9|F|A|0|2|7|

16 Narrative Statement of Facts, Conditions and Circumstances Pertinent to the Accident/Incident *(continued)*

INJURIES TO PERSONS

The pilot and one passenger sustained fatal injuries.

DAMAGE TO AIRCRAFT

The aircraft was destroyed during impact with trees and terrain.

OTHER DAMAGE

There was some damage to trees in the impact path.

CREW INFORMATION

Gilbert R. Green, age 60, held a commercial pilot's certificate number 1781635 for single engine land aircraft with instrument privileges. His second class medical had been issued on October 30, 1987, without limitation. Sources indicated he had accumulated a total of 2,680 hours at the time of the occurrence. We were unable to locate information relative to his latest biennial flight review.

AIRCRAFT INFORMATION

The aircraft, a 1971 Gulfstream AA1A (formerly Grumman/American), serial number AA1A-0096, had accumulated 1,865 hours total time and 17 hours since the last annual inspection conducted on January 12, 1988, at the time of the accident. The aircraft was maintained in accordance with existing Federal Aviation Regulations and was properly certificated for the proposed flight.

WRECKAGE/IMPACT INFORMATION

The aircraft descended into 40 to 50 foot tall trees, on a easterly heading, in what a witness indicated was a nosedown, wing level attitude. The aircraft descended progressively downward until ground impact, 276 feet east of the first impact marks on a tree. The aircraft remained intact during the impact sequence, with the exception of the right wing tip, the engine top cowling half, the canopy, and the windshield. All major components were accounted for at the impact site. All flight and engine control continuity was established. No discrepancies were found in the engine or airframe which would have contributed to the accident.

MEDICAL INFORMATION

No anomalies were found during the autopsy or toxicological findings on specimens of the pilot which would have a negative impact on the proposed flight.

Attach additional pages as necessary (Page 2a, 2b, 2c, etc.)

NTSB Form 6120.4 (Rev. 1-84)

Page 2

The dispassionate report of the National Transportation Safety Board formally summarizes the facts of the accident.

3

How Not to Trust God

The Deadly Effects of Wrong Thinking

· ·

> *Trust in the Lord with all your heart*
> *And do not lean on your own understanding.*
> *In all your ways acknowledge Him,*
> *And He will make your paths straight.*
> *(Proverbs 3:5–6)*

Nothing in my Christian life to that point had prepared me for the miry pit of heavy grief which followed.

I missed Dad. My work declined. I made life difficult for Nancy. But my worst suffering, by far, was that God had seemingly abandoned me. The early joy of my conversion was replaced with sobs and sleepless nights.

I searched my heart for unconfessed sin that might explain the lack of comfort. With Job, I prayed, "Have I sinned? What have I done to You, O watcher of men?" (Job 7:20).

Looking back on those bitter days, I think several false ideas about trusting God delayed my comfort, hindered my spiritual growth, and made a bad situation worse.

Falsehood #1:
Christians Should Not Experience Trials

Some teachers would lead you to believe that God does not want Christians to suffer trials. They say poor health, family problems, or financial difficulties show that you lack faith. But the Bible quickly exposes that lie and the false guilt it lays on sincere people in the midst of their struggles:

> Man, who is born of woman, is short-lived and full of turmoil.
> (Job 14:1)

Consider it all joy, my brethren, when you encounter various trials, knowing that the testing of your faith produces endurance.
(James 1:2–3)

In this you greatly rejoice, even though now for a little while, if necessary, you have been distressed by various trials.
(1 Peter 1:6)

Those verses, and others like them, show that a Christian should *expect* difficulties during his earthly life. They may come in different shapes and sizes, but they do come.

Falsehood #2:
If You Are Suffering, It Must Be Because You Sinned

This falsehood is a variation of the first. Some Christians assume they will avoid suffering if they live a reasonably righteous life. If a person suffers, he must have sin in his life.

In a cosmic sense, yes, all human suffering is a result of sin. When God created Adam and placed him in the Garden of Eden, Adam enjoyed unhindered fellowship with God (Gen. 2), and no pains or hardships blighted creation. Only after Adam and Eve sinned did death and suffering enter into the world (Rom. 5:12).

And in a practical sense, there is *often* a direct connection between sin and suffering. A man who sits in prison suffers as a direct result of his crimes. A woman who loses her marriage and family because of infidelity suffers as a direct result of her sins.

But there is not *always* a direct cause-and-effect relationship between one man's sin and his particular suffering. Job's "friends," for example, accused him of harboring unconfessed sin when they saw his pain (Job 4:7–8). But they misread the situation. God Himself affirmed that Job was "a blameless and upright man, fearing God and turning away from evil" (Job 1:8,

2:3). God brought suffering into Job's life to accomplish purposes other than punishing him for sin.

Still not convinced? Jesus' disciples saw a man blind from birth and assumed that either he or his parents had sinned. But Jesus told them that his blindness did not result from sin in the man or his parents (John 9:1–3). In like manner, the apostle Paul had multiple hardships in the course of his faithful ministry (2 Cor. 11:23–33), but he did not identify them as punishments for sins.

The point is clinched when we consider Christ Himself.

> Christ also suffered for you, leaving you an example for you to follow in His steps, who committed no sin, nor was any deceit found in His mouth.
> (1 Peter 2:21–22)

Christ most certainly did not sin—and yet He suffered. It is not too much for His disciples to expect that they may follow in His steps of suffering, since the disciple is not above the teacher (*cf.* John 15:18–20).

All believers suffer, but not all their suffering is a direct result of their personal sin. We live in a fallen world that will often inflict hardship apart from any moral failings of our own.

Falsehood #3:
God's Comfort Comes Automatically

Immediately after the plane crash, I expected peace like a river to attend my way.[2] I just assumed my heart would be "fully blessed, finding as He promised, perfect peace and rest."[3]
So much for basing my spiritual expectations on familiar hymns.

In the days after our family's loss, I started to pray and read the Bible, but the peaceful river didn't flow. Instead, a dark cloud descended upon my heart. Horrible nightmares

2 Cf. *When Peace Like a River* (a hymn by Horatio Gates Spafford)
3 From *Like a River Glorious* (a hymn by Frances Ridley Havergal)

disrupted my sleep. Well-intentioned but misguided friends aggravated my soul by talking too much and listening too little. Sermons instructed my head but did not comfort my heart.

I did not realize it at the time, but a profound spiritual crisis was enveloping my soul. The truth I knew was not helping me.

As it turns out, I did not know how to trust God.

In retrospect, my assumptions were all wrong. I did not understand the power of grief, and I thought God's comfort would come as I passively waited for it.

The great preacher Martyn Lloyd-Jones says that too many people think faith operates like a thermostat. You initially set the thermostat at your desired temperature. If the room gets too cold, the thermostat automatically warms the room without any thought or effort on your part. Equilibrium just happens.[4]

But faith in the Christian life does not work like that. Our minds are subject to decay. They need renewal through the Word and the Spirit.

> And do not be conformed to this world, but be transformed by the renewing of your mind, so that you may prove what the will of God is, that which is good and acceptable and perfect.
> (Rom. 12:2)

> Like newborn babies, long for the pure milk of the word, so that by it you may grow in respect to salvation.
> (1 Peter 2:2)

So, faith does not automatically give us peace in the midst of our trials. If it did, Christians would *never* be anxious or discouraged. Every Christian, without exception, would be strong and courageous as the winds of trial blew around and about. And the many New Testament passages that exhort us to faith and trust would be rendered unnecessary (e.g., Phil. 4:6–7; 1 Peter 5:6–7).

4 D. Martyn Lloyd-Jones, *Spiritual Depression: Its Causes and Cure* (Grand Rapids, MI: Eerdmans, 1987), 142–43.

No, you and I need to stir up our faith in the midst of our trials. We must remember biblical truth and rest in it if we are to know the comfort that God has promised in His Word. We can readily see this in the book of Lamentations in the Old Testament.

The prophet Jeremiah is describing the destruction of Jerusalem in 586 BC. God's hand of judgment has fallen on the sinful people. The man of God is discouraged.

> My soul has been rejected from peace; I have forgotten happiness. So I say, "My strength has perished, and so has my hope from the LORD."
> (Lam. 3:17–18)

But in the midst of that discouragement, he meditates on great truths about God and finds new hope:

> This I recall to mind, therefore I have hope. The LORD's lovingkindnesses indeed never cease, for His compassions never fail. They are new every morning. Great is Your faithfulness.
> (Lam. 3:21–23)

Jeremiah kindled faith in his soul by exercising his mind to recall truth about the attributes of God. God is a God of loyal love and enduring compassion. He never forgets His people. That means He had not forgotten Jeremiah in the midst of the fall of Jerusalem.

Jeremiah renewed his mind in the midst of his troubles by calling to mind the character of God and His faithfulness. Perhaps he had lost sight of it in the midst of the horrors around him. In any event, he reminded himself of things he had overlooked for a time. As he remembered the goodness of God, his hope was rekindled even though the circumstances had not changed.

Turning profoundly to Scripture is the key to finding that hope.

For whatever was written in earlier times was written for our instruction, so that through perseverance and the encouragement of the Scriptures we might have hope.
(Rom. 15:4)

All Scripture is inspired by God and profitable for teaching, for reproof, for correction, for training in righteousness; so that the man of God may be adequate, equipped for every good work.
(2 Tim. 3:16–17)

As an example, brethren, of suffering and patience, take the prophets who spoke in the name of the Lord. We count those blessed who endured.
(James 5:10)

A contemporary of Jeremiah by the name of Habakkuk learned this in his own spiritual experience. Habakkuk was agitated over the condition of God's people and discouraged by the Lord's seeming lack of a response to his prayers. Yet without any change in his circumstances, he went from despair to joy.

You say you've never read Habakkuk? It's time you got acquainted with his book. It will teach us this profoundly important lesson about trusting God in trying times:

You trust God when you evaluate your problems in light of His ways that He has revealed in His Word, and then place your heart confidence in Him that He will deal with you consistently with His ways.

Trusting does not begin with trying harder to believe God. That's what the misguided pastor tried to tell me in my sorrow. He was wrong.

Trusting begins with biblical thinking. You must think rightly about God and His ways with His people if you are going to find true, lasting peace in the midst of your adversity.

I'm privileged to point you in the right direction in the pages that follow.

4

Help from an Unexpected Place

About Habakkuk and the Times in Which He Lived

. . . .

For whatever was written in earlier times was written for our instruction, so that through perseverance and the encouragement of the Scriptures we might have hope.
(Romans 15:4)

The book of Habakkuk is a prophecy concerning the impending fall of Judah at the hands of the Chaldeans. It was probably written during the reign of wicked King Jehoiakim (*cf.* 2 Kings 23:31–37), when the Chaldeans were ascending to power, and sin and evil were prevalent in God's chosen nation of Judah. Habakkuk's name means "to embrace," perhaps suggesting his role as one who embraces and comforts his people in the time of their calamity.[5]

The Bible tells us that Jehoiakim was an evil king, and we get some insight into his wickedness from Jeremiah's writings.

> In the fourth year of Jehoiakim the son of Josiah, king of Judah, this word came to Jeremiah from the LORD, saying, "Take a scroll and write on it all the words which I have spoken to you concerning Israel and concerning Judah, and concerning all the nations, from the day I first spoke to you, from the days of Josiah, even to this day. Perhaps the house of Judah will hear all the calamity which I plan to bring on them, in order that every man will turn from his evil way; then I will forgive their iniquity and their sin." (Jer. 36:1–3)

God was warning of judgment but simultaneously offering forgiveness if the people would repent. What was Jehoiakim's response?

5 Charles L. Feinberg, *The Minor Prophets* (Chicago, IL: Moody Press, 1990), 205.

The king sent Jehudi to get the scroll, and he took it out
of the chamber of Elishama the scribe. And Jehudi read it
to the king as well as to all the officials who stood beside
the king. Now the king was sitting in the winter house in
the ninth month, with a fire burning in the brazier before
him. When Jehudi had read three or four columns, the
king cut it with a scribe's knife and threw it into the fire
that was in the brazier, until all the scroll was consumed
in the fire that was in the brazier. Yet the king and all his
servants who heard all these words were not afraid, nor
did they rend their garments.
(Jer. 36:21–24)

The king was so vile that he cut up the scroll containing
the message of God's judgment and threw it into the fire. What
contempt for the Word of God! It reflects the society to whom
Habakkuk wrote. Spiritual provocation was all around him,
and the wicked seemed to act with impunity.

The Chaldeans were a people that formed the dominant
population in Babylonia. Their influence was so great that the
term *Chaldean* became almost synonymous with the term *Babylonian*.

The nation of Babylon began to rise to power between 650
and 600 BC. Ultimately, King Nebuchadnezzar came against
Judah and conquered it (2 Kings 24). The Bible says God raised
Babylon into power to be an instrument of His judgment on
His disobedient people, using Nebuchadnezzar as His "servant" (*cf.* Jer. 25:8–9).

Habakkuk ministered during the simultaneous spiritual
decline of Judah and the military rise of Babylon. Inwardly,
he struggled because, from his perspective, God did not seem
concerned about the evil among His own people. Habakkuk's prayers for God's intervention were going unanswered.
Indeed, the situation was getting worse. It was a disturbing
case of divine silence.

The book of Habakkuk is the inspired account of how God
brought Habakkuk from a place of discouragement to a place

of joy—*without changing anything about the existing circumstances.* In fact, Habakkuk would actually learn that the future would be bleaker than the present. But because he learned better how to trust God, the book ends in joy, not discouragement.

The book of Habakkuk takes the form of a dialogue between the prophet and God, which we can easily trace as follows.

1.
Habakkuk speaks in 1:1–4.
Habakkuk prays to God, complaining that He had not answered his prayers to change the sinfulness of the nation.

2.
God responds to Habakkuk in 1:5–11.
God responds to Habakkuk's complaint and reveals that He is raising up the Chaldeans to judge Judah.

3.
Habakkuk replies to God in 1:12–2:1.
Habakkuk asks how God could use a wicked nation to judge His own people. He cannot reconcile God's holiness with His intended actions. After he expresses his confusion, Habakkuk waits for the Lord's answer.

4.
God speaks again in 2:2–20.
God responds by revealing that the Chaldean success will only be temporary. After they have served their purpose, God will execute judgment on them. By contrast, the righteous will live by faith (2:4).

5.
Habakkuk concludes the dialogue in 3:1–19.
Habakkuk responds with a prayer of submission and trust. He realizes the coming situation will be severe, but nevertheless he rejoices in the Lord.

As that dialogue unfolds, Habakkuk's faith matures as God reveals His ways to the prophet.

You are going to watch a soul grow before your very eyes. In the process, you will find that which gives you encouragement from the hand of God. Habakkuk was able to move from discouragement to hope because he learned how to trust God—even though nothing changed in the circumstances.

Believe me, my friend—God's help to Habakkuk will help you, too. It will help you no matter what tempts you to discouragement or despair—be it the corruption in your government, the decay in culture, unfaithfulness in the church of Christ, or the inward angst of a broken heart. The principles of how to trust God can cause your soul to grow, too.

5

God's Ways Are Not Your Ways

Habakkuk 1:1–4

. . . .

"For My thoughts are not your thoughts,
Nor are your ways My ways," declares the LORD.
"For as the heavens are higher than the earth,
So are My ways higher than your ways
And My thoughts than your thoughts."
(Isaiah 55:8–9)

One hidden challenge in our trials is coming to grips with the fact that life has disappointed our plans and hopes. We didn't get what we had our hearts set on. Habakkuk can relate.

Habakkuk's Dilemma

Habakkuk knew all about disillusionment.

> The oracle which Habakkuk the prophet saw.
> How long, O LORD, will I call for help,
> And You will not hear?
> I cry out to You, "Violence!"
> Yet You do not save.
> Why do You make me see iniquity,
> And cause me to look on wickedness?
> Yes, destruction and violence are before me;
> Strife exists and contention arises.
> Therefore the law is ignored
> And justice is never upheld.
> For the wicked surround the righteous;
> Therefore justice comes out perverted.
> (Hab. 1:1–4)

This text takes us into the prayer life of a faithful, persistent man who expects God to answer prayer. As you read those verses, you are joining Habakkuk's prayer life "in progress."

Notice how he says, "How long, O LORD, will I call for help, and You will not hear?" He sees his society filled with sin, violence, and injustice. He is disturbed because God hasn't responded to his prayers about the problem. He saw iniquity and wickedness all around him. Destruction and violence were before him, the law was being ignored, and justice was never upheld. These conditions existed among God's chosen people with no sign of change.

He knew God was a holy God who promised to bless His people when they obeyed. But when he looked around and saw the sin, he just couldn't make it all fit together. God seemed to let the problem go unchecked.

Habakkuk had been praying long enough to believe that God should have done something by now. Doesn't the effective prayer of a righteous man accomplish much (James 5:16)? Why did this evil continue? God was not meeting his spiritual expectations.

He said, in effect, "I've been praying about this problem. The situation is obviously wrong. You're a holy God who loves righteousness. Why aren't You responding?"

Habakkuk thought God should intervene and change the people, so he prayed to that end. But God let the situation worsen. He wasn't doing it Habakkuk's way.

It is humbling to realize that God has the sovereign prerogative to answer our prayers in any manner He chooses. Sometimes—if not often—it pleases Him to answer differently than we would like (*cf.* 2 Cor. 12:7–10).

We trust God in part by bowing to His sovereignty. What else could Jesus have meant when He told us to pray, "Your will be done, on earth as it is in heaven" (Matt. 6:10)?

God's Ways Are Not Your Ways

As you read this book, my friend, you may be overwhelmed by circumstances, and you find yourself becoming bewildered and discouraged. You wonder why God doesn't act to deliver you. I certainly felt that way in the aftermath of the plane crash.

But I really think it helps us to remember that God has the sovereign right to do things differently than we would have Him do them.

> "For My thoughts are not your thoughts, nor are your ways My ways," declares the LORD. "For as the heavens are higher than the earth, so are My ways higher than your ways and My thoughts than your thoughts."
> (Isa. 55:8–9)

If God is not responding to your prayers as you wish, perhaps He has a better purpose for the future than you understand now. That may be hard to hear in your discouragement, but isn't it at least possible?

I write from compassion for you and as one whose heart has been profoundly broken. It is healthy for us to say to ourselves, "Well, yes, of course I find perplexing things in my life and the world around me. Of course there are things that I would do differently. God is at work, and He thinks differently than I do. He thinks bigger than I do. He thinks *better* than I do. And He's in charge. I don't like it now, but at least I understand that everything is not spinning wildly out of control, despite appearances to the contrary."

We must remember who sits on the throne of the universe. To trust God is to submit our minds to the fact that God does things His way, not ours. To be a Christian is to yield to Christ as Lord—even when our prayers turn out differently than we had hoped.

That is foundational to trusting God.

When Prayers Seem Unanswered

A key lesson was impressed upon me in my early experience with prayer groups. Have you ever noticed that when someone comes back with a good medical report ("There's no cancer!") the response is always, "Praise God! Isn't He so good?"

But you don't have to be around too long before someone comes along with a bad report. "Bill only has a few months to live." A quiet response often seeks to avoid the awkward topic.

That's sad. Is God only gracious when someone receives a good prognosis? Does our view of God shift depending on what doctors say?

Well-meaning pastors try to motivate people by assuring them that "prayer can change things." I once heard about a man who supposedly prayed for the salvation of five friends over a period of fifty-two years. Eventually, they all came to Christ, including at least one after the praying man had died.

Now that's wonderful, but it raises the question—what about those times when a loved one does *not* come to Christ? What do we say to aging parents whose adult children have rejected Christ and have no interest in the spiritual things in which they were raised? If God does not grant the answer we seek, should we pass over it quickly and hope no one notices?

I think not. God may respond to our prayers differently than we ask in order to accomplish other purposes in us. God did not remove Paul's thorn in the flesh but instead showed him the sufficiency of His grace (*cf.* 2 Cor. 12:7–10).

My friend, the truth is that God may not answer your prayers in your way or on your timetable. He may leave you in a difficult state even though it deeply disturbs you. His reasons for that may not be discernible to you.

However, the painful edge of unanswered prayer is softened when you remember that God's ways are not your ways. That helps you persevere. God's seeming silence in your life does not mean He has abandoned you. He would never do that. He is a faithful God (*cf.* Heb. 13:5).

You can still trust God. He has His ways and His ways are

always good—even when they hurt.

Habakkuk 1:2–4 also introduces the issue of whether it is legitimate to pray prayers of complaint. Habakkuk expresses his displeasure in rather confrontational terms to God. Later in the book, he questions God even further (1:13–17).

Is such boldness an appropriate way to address almighty God? Did Habakkuk lack faith as he prayed? I certainly don't see it that way.

It was precisely because Habakkuk *did* have faith that he was disturbed in the first place. He believed in God's Word, practiced prayer, expected answers to his prayer, and hated sin. He longed for the holiness of God and the holiness of His people. When his experience did not square with his theology, it troubled Habakkuk deeply.

Yet, in the midst of his confusion, he did not quit. Instead, he wrestled with God on the issue, holding Him to His Word until He answered him. That is not a lack of faith. That is extraordinary faith.

Further, God did not reprove the prophet for the tone of his complaint. He interacted with His prophet extensively as Habakkuk tried to come to grips with God's dealings with the nation.

We need not rebuke the prophet. He prayed with a sincere heart out of concern for God, His Word, and His people. As John Calvin says, "God does not condemn this freedom in our prayers; but, on the contrary, the end of praying is, that every one of us pour forth . . . his heart before God."[6]

Habakkuk teaches us that we can come honestly and freely to God in a time of great need, expressing even complaints about His perceived dealings with us. Importantly, this invitation to bold openness is no license to irreverent prayer any more than grace is a license to sin (Rom. 6:1–2).

First Peter says you are to "cast all your anxiety upon Him,

---

6 John Calvin, *Commentaries on the Twelve Minor Prophets*, Vol. IV, Volume XV of Calvin's Commentaries (Edinburgh: Calvin Translation Society, Reprint, Grand Rapids, MI: Baker Books, 2009), 19.

because He cares for you" (1 Peter 5:7). The writer of Hebrews calls us to "draw near with confidence to the throne of grace"—why?—"that we may receive mercy and may find grace to help in time of need" (Heb. 4:15–16).

As you read this, my friend, consider this: Those promises are *worthless* if we cannot pray honestly. Besides, in His omniscience, God knows what you're thinking before you say it (Ps. 139:4). If questions fill your heart, you may as well spill them out before God in the privacy of your prayer closet. Is this not His explicit invitation?

> Trust in Him at all times, O people; pour out your heart before Him; God is a refuge for us.
> (Ps. 62:8)

Our union with Christ gives us the freedom to pour out our hearts before God and to trust that He will respond with the care and affection of a heavenly Father. If you're overwhelmed by circumstances, you trust God in part by taking your burdens honestly to God.

He is ultimately the only one that can give strength to your soul and lead you out of the spiritual difficulty you're facing.

> I cry aloud with my voice to the LORD . . . I pour out my complaint before Him; I declare my trouble before Him.
> (Ps. 142:1–2)

Not everyone will experience this kind of spiritual trauma. But for those who do, Christ has loved us with a breadth and length and height and depth of extraordinary love (*cf.* Eph. 3:18–19). The weary and heavy-laden can go to Him for mercy without fear (Matt. 11:28–30).

If that was all that Habakkuk had to teach us, we would have benefitted immensely.

But we have barely started. There's so much more to see about trusting God.

6

God's Ways Are Often Hidden

Habakkuk 1:5–11

. . . .

The secret things belong to the LORD our God, but the things revealed belong to us and to our sons forever, that we may observe all the words of this law.
(Deuteronomy 29:29)

God had heard Habakkuk's prayers. Now in gracious condescension, in wonderful faithfulness, God engages the prayers of a complaining prophet.

The Lord's response is recorded in 1:5–11. While there is no indication how long He waited before answering the prophet, at some point He broke His silence and revealed His perspective and future intentions for Judah. Contrary to Habakkuk's complaint that He was not responding to the situation, God states that He is actively accomplishing His own purpose.

> "Look among the nations! Observe!
> Be astonished! Wonder!
> Because I am doing something in your days—
> You would not believe if you were told.
> "For behold, I am raising up the Chaldeans,
> That fierce and impetuous people
> Who march throughout the earth
> To seize dwelling places which are not theirs."
> (Hab. 1:5–6)

Specifically, He is raising up the Chaldeans—a ruthless nation—to discipline Judah for the sin of which Habakkuk complained. God reveals that He was moving among the nations so as to bring Judah into subjection to a foreign power. Not only was God not indifferent, but He was working out an answer to the problem on an astonishing scale that far exceeded anything that Habakkuk could have anticipated. The invaders would be powerful, well-armed, and dangerous (1:6–10). They would come against Judah and prevail.

In essence, God told Habakkuk to look out at the world scene. The power that was on the rise had a specific purpose in the plan of God. They would conquer His own people and carry them into exile.

In holy tenderness, God told Habakkuk that he saw only part of the picture. God was more concerned about the sin of His people than he was. He was raising up a new world power to correct the very sin problem that Habakkuk had rightly identified. They would invade Judah as His instrument of judgment.

Habakkuk had wrongly judged the situation in his opening prayer. Crucial matters were outside the range of his comprehension. God was actually *at that time* working out His eternal purpose in a way that was far greater than Habakkuk could have asked or thought (*cf.* Eph. 3:20).

The power that was on the rise had a specific purpose in the plan of God. It would sweep through Judah.

That was God's response to the sin of His people. He controls the rise and fall of nations (Dan. 2:21). God was going to use that wicked nation to be an instrument of His judgment.

> "Then they will sweep through like the wind and pass on.
> But they will be held guilty,
> They whose strength is their god."
> (Hab. 1:11)

Habakkuk had a limited perspective. He had seen only the visible situation going from bad to worse. He did not see—and could not see—that God was adjusting the world order to address the situation Habakkuk was concerned about.

God was letting Habakkuk in on His hidden ways—the manner in which He directs all creatures and events to accomplish His will. We call that His providence. In an invisible way, God works out His purpose in everything that happens in the heavens and on the earth (*cf.* Eph. 1:11).

My friend, that means God is always doing more in your life than you can see from your limited perspective. When your circumstances seem very negative, remind yourself that you don't know the whole story. In fact, you don't know *most* of the story—just as Habakkuk didn't know the whole story in his opening prayer.

There are things beyond your comprehension, which, if you knew them, would immediately show that God has perfect control of your situation. The problem is not with God; it's that you see only part of the picture. Because God works "behind the scenes," you are not in a position to make a final evaluation about your present circumstances. A familiar Bible passage teaches us that very point:

> Trust in the LORD with all your heart
> And do not lean on your own understanding.
> In all your ways acknowledge Him,
> And He will make your paths straight.
> (Prov. 3:5–6)

How can you trust God in your trying times, then? You need to trust God more than you trust your own judgment. He works in astonishing ways that you cannot perceive. His providential dealings may be hidden, but they are certain.

Beloved, God unfolds His work in your life over time. His hidden ways are at work in every detail of your life, even if you don't recognize it at the present. He is working it all out for His glory and your good. In the midst of trials, you trust God by *giving Him time to prove His faithfulness to you.* It may be bleak for years. But you don't know how it's going to work out in the end.

We are not in a position to judge the ways of God in this life. We only see through a veil darkly.

Rather than rely on *our* judgment to evaluate what's happening, we must trust the character of God and say, "God, I don't see it all, but I know who You are. I'm content to rest in that, even when I don't understand my circumstances."

God causes all things to work together for good to those
who love God and are called according to His purpose.
(Rom. 8:28)

Trust believes God will vindicate His faithfulness and goodness in the end. I say it gently: Life may be breaking your heart
just now, my friend, but you don't have to understand if you
belong to Christ. The triune God holds you in His hand (John
10:27–29) and keeps your tears in a bottle lest they be forgotten
(*cf.* Ps. 56:8). That is enough.

Because God's ways are usually hidden from your view,
what you see now is not a reliable indicator of what is good.
You must trust Him more than you trust yourself.

You can do that when you embrace God's hidden ways. You
can say, "Though I am discouraged and broken, I will give God
time to show His faithfulness to me. I am certain He will do
good to me in the end."

That's an important part of trusting God.

7

God's Ways Are Holy

Habakkuk 1:12–17
· · · · · · · · · · · · · · · · ·

And one called out to another and said,
"Holy, Holy, Holy, is the Lord of hosts,
The whole earth is full of His glory."
(Isaiah 6:3)

Good/Bad Quiz

I have a quiz for you as we begin this chapter. It's like a true/false quiz, except this is a good/bad quiz. I'll describe a situation, and you decide whether it's good or bad. Here are some real-life examples.

- A Middle Eastern family sells one of its children into slavery because he is a believer. Is that a good thing or a bad thing?
- A godly man, through no fault of his own, has no food or shelter in the midst of terribly cold weather. Is that a good thing or a bad thing?
- An innocent man is executed for crimes he did not commit on the basis of false testimony. Is that a good thing or a bad thing?

Your first impulse on those questions would be to say that those things were *bad* things. The Middle Eastern man did no wrong. The godly man deserves a better life. Innocent people should not be executed for crimes they did not commit.

In every example, you would be wrong.

The man sold into slavery was Joseph in the book of Genesis. The Bible says that when his brothers sold him into captivity, God meant it for good (Gen. 50:20).

The man in suffering was the apostle Paul. He said that

when he suffered lack in his apostolic ministry, God was perfecting His strength in Paul's weakness (2 Cor. 12:9–10).

And who was the innocent man executed on false testimony? The Lord Jesus Christ, the perfect Son of God, when He was crucified at Calvary to pay the penalty for sin. God was carrying out His predetermined plan of salvation which He established before the foundation of the world (Acts 2:23).

God was doing good things, although your initial impression based on limited information was that they were bad things. Here's what I want you to see. It's very crucial for trusting God in trying times.

When you have limited information and a limited perspective, your judgment is *unreliable*. You have an unwarranted bias in favor of your own opinion. We are all subject to jumping to conclusions before we have all the facts. Scripture warns us against that tendency.

> He who gives an answer before he hears, it is folly and shame to him.
> (Prov. 18:13)

We need to carry that recognition into the way we evaluate the circumstances in our lives. When difficult things happen in the world or in our personal lives, we have to remember that we are not in a position to make ultimate judgments about what is good and bad.

What shall we rely upon if not our own judgment? The answer to that question helps us understand better how to trust God.

In 1:12–2:1, Habakkuk replies to God's initial revelation to him. God's answer clarified some things but also created even more difficult questions for him. Now the prophet must wrestle with the issue of how a holy God could use wicked people to accomplish His good purposes.

God had just told him that exile was coming. Life as Habakkuk had known it would come to an end. The prophet staggered under the weight of the announcement and had to find some spiritual footing.

It would be like Americans hearing that Islamic fundamentalists would come to conquer the United States. Christianity would be outlawed and Sharia Law imposed on an unwilling nation. That level of terror measures what the Chaldeans were bringing to Judah. Ruthless and violent, they had no regard for the people of God.

So Habakkuk talks with God and reasons with his own soul. He does not express his new questions immediately. Rather, he remembers God's character, draws certain conclusions from there, and *only then* expresses his further questions. Look at how he prays:

> Are You not from everlasting,
> O LORD, my God, my Holy One?
> We will not die.
> You, O LORD, have appointed them to judge;
> And You, O Rock, have established them to correct.
> Your eyes are too pure to approve evil,
> And You can not look on wickedness with favor.
> Why do You look with favor
> On those who deal treacherously?
> Why are You silent when the wicked swallow up
> Those more righteous than they?
> (Hab. 1:12–13)

The *method* of his thinking is critical. Before he considers his new problem, he rehearses the character of God in prayer. He says, "God, You are holy and everlasting. Whatever these circumstances mean, they cannot mean the end of our nation, because *that* would mean that You had not been true to Your character."

Habakkuk builds a spiritual framework within which to think. God's holy and faithful character means He would never abandon His people. So whatever else the coming invasion meant, it would not spell the final and absolute extermination of God's people. God's holiness performed a negative function by showing what these new developments could *not* mean.

Everlasting indicates God is the eternal One who has always existed and ruled over all. *Holy One* emphasizes God's moral purity. God could never do anything wrong or contrary to His nature.

Habakkuk doesn't yet understand God's ultimate purpose in raising up the Chaldeans, but he knows that God had promised a seed to Abraham and a throne to David's descendants (Gen. 12:3; 2 Sam. 7).

Habakkuk stood in the lineage of those promises. God's faithfulness meant He would never break those promises. He is a God of truth who can never lie (*cf.* Titus 1:2). The coming Chaldeans could never cancel the promises of God

In effect, Habakkuk says, "Even though it looks like the Chaldeans will exterminate us, that cannot possibly be the final outcome. God must have another end in mind with this coming invasion."

How does that help you and me? Habakkuk's method teaches us how to reason about our sorrows from a New Testament perspective. Consider these two verses.

In this is love, not that we loved God but that He loved us and gave His Son to be the propitiation for our sins.
(1 John 4:10)

And He will wipe away every tear from their eyes; and there will no longer be any death; there will no longer be any mourning, or crying, or pain; the first things have passed away.
(Rev. 21:4)

Christian friend, God has proven His perfect love for you when Jesus Christ died for your sins on the cross. In the future, He will comfort you so perfectly that tears and death will be no more. Let that settle in.

If Christ loved you enough to shed His blood for you, you know that His love has not ceased simply because adversity has come to you. Surely the intentions of the One who suffered for you are good. Yes, you may know pain now, but God promises to remove all pain in heaven. As difficult as life's misery may be, it is only temporary. Even death itself will be swallowed up in victory (*cf.* 1 Cor. 15:54).

I understand that those truths do not explain or solve your immediate problem. But they do something even more important. They give you a clear context in which to think about your present pain. If you are a Christian, God loves you with a faithful love. He will do good to you—you just don't see it yet. Based on the greater things He has done in Christ at the cross, and based on the greater things He will do in heaven, you can trust Him for the lesser things of this earthly life that occur in between. The cross and heaven are unanswerable arguments for the love of God and His good purpose for your life.

The example of Habakkuk calls you to recite truth in your heart. As you do, the Holy Spirit will, in time, produce a sense of trust that enables you to overcome your present heartaches. He will teach you not to question God's character or the goodness of His intentions toward you. You will find that you actually do trust Him even though life is difficult. You first think about what is true. Then peace follows.

> Finally, brethren, whatever is true, whatever is honorable, whatever is right, whatever is pure, whatever is lovely, whatever is of good repute, if there is any excellence and if anything worthy of praise, dwell on these things. The things you have learned and received and heard and seen in me, practice these things, and the God of peace will be with you.
> (Phil. 4:8–9)

Do you see how vastly different that is from saying in a spirit of resignation and defeat, "Yes, God's in control, but I don't understand. Why do I even bother? (Sigh.) What will be will be"?

Such defeated resignation is not worthy of Christ. It shows no confidence in His good purpose. It does not glorify God and it will discourage you. It's the wrong approach. True faith understands that God is in control, and it goes further to say that *He exercises that control in a manner that is consistent with His other attributes.*

God is sovereign *and* He is holy. God is sovereign *and* He is good. God is sovereign *and* He is faithful. When you understand His sovereignty in light of His other attributes, it lays a foundation to change the whole attitude of your heart. He will exercise His control to bless you in the end, no matter how bad it seems at the moment.

You have confidence in the outcome because you have confidence in the God who has revealed Himself in Christ and in the Bible. So you say to yourself something like this:

> Whatever else is happening to me, it cannot mean that God is being unfair or unkind to me. That would contradict His character. It cannot mean that God has abandoned me. God does not do such things. No, God is in control and God is good. Somehow, in a way that I do not understand, these circumstances further express His goodness to me, because He could not violate His faithfulness to me.

As you exercise your faith like that, Christ stands ready to help you as you call upon Him.

> For we do not have a high priest who cannot sympathize with our weaknesses, but One who has been tempted in all things as we are, yet without sin. Therefore let us draw near with confidence to the throne of grace, so that we may receive mercy and find grace to help in time of need. (Heb. 4:15–16)

Do you see how that approach changes your perspective? Even without a change in your circumstances, you can face your trials from a position of strength. You can trust God in a way that is worthy of Christ. Your heart has a true basis to rest in Him. In this manner, eternal truth is brought directly to bear on your life. It may not answer all the questions, and you may have to apply the method repeatedly, but now you have a place on which to stand.

Yet, as you read on in the first chapter of Habakkuk, you find that this approach does not make the issues simple. Sometimes, meditation on God's character leads us into even more difficult questions.

On a horizontal level, Habakkuk now understood that his people would survive the coming invasion. But that left a vertical question about the ways of God. How could a holy God use a *wicked* nation to advance His righteous purpose with His people? Look at the last part of verse 13.

> Why do You look with favor on those who deal treacherously? Why are You silent when the wicked swallow up those more righteous than they?
> (Hab. 1:13)

It was no longer just a national dilemma. It was a theological dilemma. How could God strengthen a nation more wicked than His own people to prevail over them? How is that consistent with His own holiness? He summarizes the difficulty in verse 17.

> Will they therefore empty their net and continually slay nations without sparing?
> (Hab. 1:17)

Habakkuk shows us that the man of faith does not have to hide his questions. He asks them in reverence and he looks to the Word of God to find his answers. Further study, further meditation, and further illumination from the Holy Spirit may bring resolution in time.

The key is to recognize that important spiritual principles are not gained or understood in a moment. It takes patience. It takes time. It may continue to be difficult.

Do you want to trust God and know Him in your trying times? Call to mind His holy, faithful character. Remember the person and work of Jesus Christ. Anticipate your future in heaven.

And what if you have done all that and you still face questions that trouble you deeply? Keep reading, my friend.

8

God's Ways May Make You Wait

Habakkuk 2:1
· · · · · · · · · · · · · · ·

*Wait for the L*ORD*;*
Be strong and let your heart take courage;
*Yes, wait for the L*ORD*.*
(Psalm 27:14)

Trials can last a long time. It took me several years to sort through all that was on my heart after the plane crash. It was so difficult that at one point I considered dropping out of seminary. How could I call people to trust God when I had doubts of my own?

As you move into chapter 2 of Habakkuk, you find some perspective for chronic trials that seem to linger over your life. Remember, Habakkuk had just asked how God could use a wicked nation to advance His purposes with His own people. There was no ready answer. So what did he do? We find it in 2:1.

> I will stand on my guard post
> And station myself on the rampart;
> And I will keep watch to see what He will speak to me,
> And how I may reply when I am reproved.
> (Hab. 2:1)

Habakkuk now compares himself to the watchman who looks for movement on the horizon. In the day, watchmen kept watch from city walls, watchtowers, or hilltops for any sign of activity that might affect the inhabitants.

Part of their duty was to watch for runners who would be bringing messages for the king (*cf.* 2 Sam. 18:24–27). No doubt there were times of watching when nothing happened. But the first sign of motion could be significant. The watchman's duty was to keep a vigilant eye for developments.

It's not that Habakkuk literally went up to a watchtower. He simply prepared his heart to watch for God's answer to him. He knew God *could* answer. He knew God *would* answer. So, as it were, he looked expectantly to the horizon as he anticipated the response of God to his questions.

Habakkuk has laid down eternal absolutes and expressed his questions about the Lord's dealings, but he still has no answer or resolution to his problem. Notice that he does not give up in despair or turn away from God over his apparently unsolvable dilemma.

Rather, knowing that an all-wise God has an answer, Habakkuk commits his problem to God and simply waits for a reply. His questions are finished. Now it's simply time to wait.

Scripture counsels us to be patient in our trials.

> Teach me Your way, O LORD,
> And lead me in a level path
> Because of my foes.
> Do not deliver me over to the desire of my adversaries,
> For false witnesses have risen against me,
> And such as breathe out violence.
> I would have despaired unless I had believed that I would
> see the goodness of the LORD
> In the land of the living.
> Wait for the LORD;
> Be strong and let your heart take courage;
> Yes, wait for the LORD.
> (Ps. 27:11–14)

> Yet those who wait for the LORD
> Will gain new strength;
> They will mount up with wings like eagles,
> They will run and not get tired,
> They will walk and not become weary.
> (Isa. 40:31)

Biblical waiting is *not* passive resignation to the inevitable.

"God's going to do what He's going to do, so I might as well sit down and wait for Him to do it."

No, waiting is an expectant looking to God. It is not merely waiting to see what happens, but by faith, having confidence that God will answer and show His faithfulness to you. Admittedly, this cuts against the grain of our culture, which expects immediate access to everything on our smartphones and quick service in the fast-food drive-through.

But God doesn't deal with us according to the timetable of our culture. He may make us wait.

How can you trust God in your adversity? Waiting is part of the process. When the answers aren't apparent, don't panic. Don't turn to worldly counsel. Don't complain.

Instead, adopt a posture of humility in which you remain faithful in the Word and in prayer, even when it seems like it isn't making any difference. Faith looks to God and patiently waits for Him to act on His timetable. Faith says reverently, "God, You're in charge here. I don't understand, but I'll wait. I know You'll bless that persistent faith in the end." You trust God with patient endurance in the confident hope that He will eventually act decisively to deliver you.

Dear friend, even if you have to wait a long time—I suffered for seven years in that spiritual affliction—and even if it's not until you get to heaven, you will eventually see that God has fulfilled His promise of faithfulness to you. It could be no other way. He never abandons His children.

A believer in Christ must develop patience in his trials. He needs to be satisfied not to have the answers he wants. It's enough to find contentment in the context of God's holiness and the eternal love of Christ. His grace is sufficient for us, even if our prayers go unanswered (*cf.* 2 Cor. 12:7–10).

I understand that the wait seems intolerable in the moment. But let me encourage you: you can wait. We don't need answers on our timetable. We simply need to know Christ by faith. We need the power of His resurrection and the fellowship of His sufferings (Phil. 3:9–10). Those great spiritual realities can sustain your heart *even though important issues in your life are unsettled.*

True faith does not withhold worship until we figure the situation out. True faith worships God, even when we do not have a solution. Our worship of this glorious God is unconditional. It is independent of our circumstances.

> In this you greatly rejoice, even though now for a little while, if necessary, you have been distressed by various trials, so that the proof of your faith, being more precious than gold which is perishable, even though tested by fire, may be found to result in praise and glory and honor at the revelation of Jesus Christ; and though you have not seen Him, you love Him, and though you do not see Him now, but believe in Him, you greatly rejoice with joy inexpressible and full of glory, obtaining as the outcome of your faith the salvation of your souls.
> (1 Peter 1:6–9)

Are you facing trials? Are you concerned about the direction of world events? Consider God's ways. They are not your ways. They are often hidden from your eyes. They are holy.

And if you still don't understand after considering those great biblical principles, don't give up. Follow Habakkuk's example and wait with a confident expectation that God will answer you, even if you can't see how He possibly could.

His deliverance may come in ways that you do not see coming. He may direct your paths in a way that is completely different from what you originally wanted. But trust Him, my Christian friend, with a confidence that He will be faithful to you in the end. Your God *will* be faithful.

Just you wait and see.

9

God's Ways Are Still Future

Habakkuk 2:2–20
. . . .

For the earth will be filled
With the knowledge of the glory of the LORD,
As the waters cover the sea.
(Habakkuk 2:14)

One of the darker aspects of discouragement is that we tend to think there's no hope in the future. Tomorrow must certainly be like today, and since today is bad, tomorrow will be, also.

Christians should not let themselves think like that. It is essential that we remember the future as we think about today. And that's not just the future of the next twenty-four hours—but the entire future of God's eternal purpose for the world and for the church of Christ. God's work extends beyond our lifetimes. We must take that into account as we trust Him. That's the lesson we find in the remainder of Habakkuk 2.

Habakkuk's question (in Hab. 1:17) had been this: "Will they continually slay nations without sparing? Will they always prevail, despite their wickedness?"

His question had no immediate answer. As we saw in the last chapter, Habakkuk adopted a posture of waiting for the Lord's response (2:1). Now, God, in His faithfulness, answers the waiting prophet.

> Then the LORD answered me and said, "Record the vision and inscribe it on tablets, that the one who reads it may run. For the vision is yet for the appointed time; it hastens toward the goal and it will not fail. Though it tarries, wait for it; for it will certainly come, it will not delay."
> (Hab. 2:2–3)

In those verses, God emphasizes the importance and the

future-focused reality of what He is about to say. He tells Habakkuk to write it all down so it could be spread to others. God wanted His people to know that more was coming in the future than what they saw in the present. It was worth waiting for, even if it was delayed for an extended period of time.

God lays down a principle for the ages on dealing with the matter of spiritual life.

> Behold, as for the proud one,
> His soul is not right within him;
> But the righteous will live by his faith.
> (Hab. 2:4)

We'll focus on the first half of this verse for now, and come back to the second half later in this chapter.

What is God saying here? The pride of the wicked will lead to his undoing. God knew the Chaldeans were a boastful, evil people. That pride would be the seed of their own destruction. God governs the universe by a principle that spells ultimate doom to arrogant men.

> God is opposed to the proud, but gives grace to the humble.
> (James 4:6; *cf.* Ps. 138:6; 1 Peter 5:5.)

The prosperity of the wicked is always temporary. Unless they repent, God will bring judgment on *them*. To emphasize this point, He pronounces a series of five woes against the Chaldeans, each of which emphasizes different ways in which they were sinning against God (2:6b, 9, 12, 15, 19).

- (2:6b) Woe to him who increases what is not his—for how long—and makes himself rich with loans?
- (2:9) Woe to him who gets evil gain for his house to put his nest on high, to be delivered from the hand of calamity!
- (2:12) Woe to him who builds a city with bloodshed and founds a town with violence!

- (2:15) Woe to you who make your neighbors drink, who mix in your venom even to make them drunk so as to look on their nakedness!
- (2:19) Woe to him who says to a piece of wood, "Awake!" To a mute stone, "Arise!" And that is your teacher? Behold, it is overlaid with gold and silver, and there is no breath inside it.

God's warning to the Chaldeans is summarized in this verse:

You will be filled with disgrace rather than honor. Now you yourself drink and expose your own nakedness. The cup in the LORD's right hand will come around to you, and utter disgrace will come upon your glory. (Hab. 2:16)

The Chaldeans were like people who make themselves seem rich through the use of credit. It's only an appearance. Eventually the debt of sin owed to God has to be paid.

While their violence, perversion, and idolatry seemed to be ascendant in Habakkuk's day, such sinfulness guaranteed their ultimate downfall after a brief time of prosperity. God's wrath would certainly come around to them. All the wickedness that was driving their success would come back on their own heads.

History tells us that the Chaldeans prospered for about seventy years. Then they were conquered by the Persians. God had set predetermined limits on their success.

God's people survive. Their enemies do not. Injustice is ultimately temporary. God will do right in the end.

Habakkuk had his answer. He now understands that he must look beyond present appearances to the ultimate outcome that God would surely bring to pass.

Yet this second chapter is more than a prophecy of judgment. It is also a promise of blessing that will be fulfilled in Christ. Observe 2:4 again:

Behold, as for the proud one,
His soul is not right within him;
But the righteous will live by his faith.
(Hab. 2:4)

God calls Habakkuk to trust His Word more than he trusts what he sees. Faith believes the Word of God and acts upon it. Stated differently, faith submits to what God has said and shapes its entire view of life and the surrounding world by it. Martyn Lloyd-Jones says:

> We must ask ourselves, as in the presence of God, the simple questions: Is my life based on the faith principle? Am I submitting myself to the fact that what I read in the Bible is the Word of God and is true? And am I willing to stake everything, my life included, upon this fact? For "the just shall live by faith."[7]

My friend, that is how you trust God in trying times. You believe His Word and commit yourself to Christ even when everything on earth seems to contradict your confidence in Him. He will do good in the future even if it does not seem possible in the present.

God honors those who are faithful to Him. He follows a just principle in dealing with people and nations based on their relationship to Him. Those who are faithful will flourish in the end, even though the situation and outcomes may seem to be reversed for the time being. (Cf. Ps. 73.)

The object of our hope lies outside of us, not inside us.

Incidentally, Habakkuk 2:4 is a verse of great significance in the New Testament explanation of the gospel.

> For I am not ashamed of the gospel, for it is the power of God for salvation to everyone who believes, to the Jew first and also to the Greek. For in it the righteousness of

---

7 D. Martyn Lloyd-Jones, *From Fear to Faith: Studies in the Book of Habakkuk* (Grand Rapids, MI: Baker Book House, 1982), 53.

God is revealed from faith to faith; as it is written, "but the righteous man shall live by faith."
(Rom. 1:16–17)

Now that no one is justified by the Law before God is evident; for, "the righteous man shall live by faith."
(Gal. 3:11)

We receive salvation by faith alone in Christ alone. God declares us righteous based on the righteousness of Christ, received by faith, and not on the basis of any works we have done. We are united to Christ by faith, not by works; once saved, we live life based on a principle of faith in Him. In both instances, we commit ourselves to God in Christ based entirely on what He has said, not on anything we have done.

It's not that we put our faith in Christ and then do good works to somehow maintain our standing with God. No, by faith we trust in Christ alone. We don't add anything to His person and work to improve or maintain our standing before a holy God. Our faith is in the righteousness of Christ, not self.

True faith is a governing dynamic in the way we live our lives. True Christians live differently than we did before Christ saved us. Scripture describes conversion as a new birth (*cf.* John 3:3). God gives us new life in Christ (*cf.* 2 Cor. 5:17). The new heart we receive turns from our prior love of sin and embraces a love for righteousness. It's a complete change in which the old man dies and the new man now lives (*cf.* Col. 3:9–10).

Part of that change is trusting God in trying times—trusting Him when you don't understand, trusting Him when you don't see the answer, trusting Him even when you are crushed with disappointment and see no way forward in your grief.

And yet faith goes further. Biblical faith expects God ultimately to reverse the entire present human condition. In the midst of the woes pronounced against the Chaldeans, God tells Habakkuk:

For the earth will be filled with the knowledge of the
glory of the LORD, as the waters cover the sea.
(Hab. 2:14)

The time will come when Christ reigns on the earth, and all
nations will see Him reigning over them in glory. The time will
come when every knee will bow before Him and acknowledge
that Jesus Christ is Lord to the glory of God the Father (Phil.
2:9). Everything in the universe is moving toward the fulfillment of God's purpose.

That has a momentous impact on trusting God in trying times.

Christian friend, we will be with Christ on that glorious
day when He reigns. We will see Him face-to-face. We will
be made like Him (*cf.* 1 John 3:2). When that time comes, our
prior earthly sorrows will be swallowed up in utter victory.
The surpassing future greatness of seeing Christ face-to-face
will make past earthly matters fade into utter insignificance.

For our citizenship is in heaven, from which also we
eagerly wait for a Savior, the Lord Jesus Christ, who will
transform the body of our humble state into conformity
with the body of His glory, by the exertion of the power
that He has even to subject all things to Himself.
(Phil. 3:20–21)

For here we do not have a lasting city, but we are seeking
the city which is to come.
(Heb. 13:14)

We must take the long view in adversity. There is more to
life than what is happening *today*. God will unfold His purpose in the future. As He does, He will show that His manifold
wisdom and love were *always* at work. He never once abandoned us—even if we couldn't see His hand at the time. We
walk by faith as we look to things that are yet to come (*cf.* 2 Cor.
5:7), rather than yielding to despondency based on things in
the present. God sees not only our lives, but all of human his-

tory from beginning to end, and He actively directs all points in between (*cf.* Eph. 1:11).

> Remember the former things long past, for I am God, and there is no other; I am God, and there is no one like Me, declaring the end from the beginning, and from ancient times things which have not been done, saying, "My purpose will be established, and I will accomplish all My good pleasure."
> (Isa. 46:9–10)

I know by experience that simply trusting God may be the hardest thing of all when your world has seemingly collapsed. But I have come to understand that the Holy Spirit strengthens our faith when we remember God's future purpose for His people.

Perhaps you have heard the phrase, "This, too, shall pass." It's designed to keep us from overreacting to what is happening in the moment.

But the Christian perspective goes much further. As a Christian, you can say, "This will pass because I am a child of God. God will prove faithful to me in the end."

The best of what God is to do is still to come. And we know more today than Habakkuk did. Consider these words of Jesus:

> Do not let your heart be troubled; believe in God, believe also in Me. In My Father's house are many dwelling places; if it were not so, I would have told you; for I go to prepare a place for you. If I go and prepare a place for you, I will come again and receive you to Myself, that where I am, there you may be also.
> (John 14:1–3)

Or these words near the close of Scripture:

> And He will wipe away every tear from their eyes; and there will no longer be any death; there will no longer

be any mourning, or crying, or pain; the first things have
passed away.
(Rev. 21:4)

Knowing this, true faith can be content even in adversity
because a better, eternal future is coming.

For momentary, light affliction is producing for us an
eternal weight of glory far beyond all comparison, while
we look not at the things which are seen, but at the things
which are not seen, for the things which are seen are
temporal, but the things which are not seen are eternal.
(2 Cor. 4:17–18)

You trust God by having confidence in the plans of God,
knowing that one day God *will* prevail, He *will* do good to you
in the end, He *will* defeat wickedness permanently, and Jesus
Christ *will* abolish death. All that distracts and discourages us
in this life *will* be abolished forever. That is what we're waiting
for. The ups and downs of this life can come and go as they may.

With that in mind, God gives His final word in the dialogue
with Habakkuk:

But the Lord is in His holy temple.
Let all the earth be silent before Him.
(Hab. 2:20)

Those closing words in Habakkuk 2 cause us to look up.
When we do, we realize God is reigning in majesty over the
nations and over the details of our individual lives. He accom-
plishes His will despite all human opposition.

God is eternal and righteous in all His ways. He knows the
beginning from the end. He directs all things to accomplish
His sovereign purpose. He will punish the godless and reward
the righteous. His glory is so brilliant that no man can see Him
and live. His greatness should hush both the pagan and the
believer who question Him.

When we see those transcendent truths, we realize it is time simply to be quiet. We put aside our questions and acknowledge the God of the Bible to be sovereign over all.

Martyn Lloyd-Jones said:

> There must be no querying, no questioning, no uncertainty about the goodness and the holiness and the power of God. Do not complainingly ask, "Why does God allow this?" or "Why does God do that?" Consider the Word of the Lord to His prophet. Look up to God. Look at the ultimate and the absolute. Then let us put our hands upon our mouths that are so ready to speak foolishly. Let us realize that He is there in the temple of the universe, God over all. Let us silently humble ourselves and bow down before Him and worship Him. Let us magnify His grace, His might, His power, His goodness, and in quiet peace of heart and mind and soul wait for Him.[8]

His ways are beyond us. We cannot evaluate in time what He has purposed to last through eternity. But we do know He is great and He is good. The earth will be filled with His glory. We can dry our tears, compose our souls, and put our complaints to rest. Look beyond your present circumstances. The best is yet to come. If you are a Christian, your God-ordained destiny leads to eternal glory in Christ.

8 Lloyd-Jones, *From Fear to Faith*, 56.

10

God's Ways Call for Complete Submission

Habakkuk 3:1–2

· · · · · · · · · · · · · · · ·

Your kingdom come.
Your will be done,
On earth as it is in heaven.
(Matthew 6:10)

Habakkuk has received a staggering vision. He sees God as greater than he saw Him before, and now he knows that life in his own country will almost cease to exist. It's worse than he thought. But he submits.

> A prayer of Habakkuk the prophet, according to Shigionoth. LORD, I have heard the report about You and I fear. O LORD, revive Your work in the midst of the years, in the midst of the years make it known; In wrath remember mercy.
> (Hab. 3:1–2)

As we come to this prayer in chapter 3, we must remember that no circumstances have changed from chapter 1. Not only was Judah sinful, but a ruthless nation was coming to bring judgment upon the people and carry them into exile. God was doing something contrary to Habakkuk's original desires. That is extremely important as we read this prayer.

In chapter 3, Habakkuk is not praying in the spirit of complaint that opened the book.

Now he prays, "God, I understand what You're going to do. I fear, but I submit."

He makes no appeal to avoid the harsh consequences of national sin. He does not ask for a change in circumstances. He rests utterly on the bare Word of God and His revealed mercy to sustain him in what is to come.

He had just heard about a coming invader brought in by

the hand of God. His people were still full of wickedness. God wasn't sending revival; He was sending judgment. And yet, because Habakkuk had worked through God's hidden, holy, and future ways, he could pray with submission.

Habakkuk now understands the purpose of God. It fills him with fear. The thought of foreign invaders taking over the land was fearsome, but he even more greatly feared the Lord. It was the beginning of wisdom for him (*cf.* Prov. 9:10).

Habakkuk understands that judgment is coming. In humble submission to the Lord, he recognizes that God's judgment is right. His ways are holy. He could never do anything wrong. Habakkuk appeals not for a change in circumstance but for God to tinge His judgment with mercy.

That is our pattern for trusting God. We acknowledge the rightness of God's ways, even if they are difficult, and simply ask for grace to live in the midst of our trials. When we see things clearly, we know that we do not need an external change to bring internal contentment. It is enough to be in Christ and have His grace to live in what He has appointed for us. That supernatural attitude honors God.

There may be a struggle to get to that point, but, as we deal with trials, settled contentment is our goal. To reach it, we stay in His Word, pray through our trials, and trust the Holy Spirit to work in our hearts as we seek to do God's will (*cf.* Phil. 2:12–13). Circumstances become less important to us than knowing Christ and the character of God.

This is a key point that God wants us to come to as we deal with difficult trials. Eventually, you and I need to move beyond complaining prayer to a point where we acknowledge the rightness of God's ways—even if they are difficult—and simply ask Him for grace to live under the trial.

As we live in that humble submission, we will stop wishing life was different. We recognize that God has sovereignly and wisely ordained our position in life, we accept it, and we manifest our trust by expressing joy instead of complaint.

My friend, this all means that your circumstances do not need to change in order for you to have peace. The Word of

God is sufficient to restore your soul (*cf.* Ps. 19:7–9). It can make you adequate for every good work in the life God has given to you (2 Tim. 3:16–17). As you turn to the written Word, it will point you to the Living Word—Christ Himself—and His love for your soul. You submit trustingly to His wisdom even if He has ordered your circumstances in a way that you would not have initially chosen.

For Habakkuk, the time for disputing has passed. He has abandoned self and prefers the ways of God to life itself. A wicked nation is about to sweep through his homeland, and he doesn't breathe a word of prayer against it, because he knows it's God's way. He prefers God's will to anything else.

So he prays, *"Revive Your work."* Habakkuk asks that God, when the judgment is severe, would revive the work He had been doing among His people for centuries. At that future point, he asks God to show that He is not through with them. He pleads with God to remember mercy as judgment unfolds.

He does not pray that God would change His mind about the coming judgment. To the contrary, Habakkuk *accepts* it. This is a significant turning point for the prophet. His mouth is no longer filled with complaints. He shuts himself up completely to the character of God. Habakkuk could trust God in light of his knowledge of the ways of God. This echoes what New Testament writers said:

> I have learned to be content in whatever circumstances I am.
> (Phil. 4:11)

> Make sure that your character is free from the love of money, being content with what you have; for He Himself has said, "I will never desert you, nor will I ever forsake you."
> (Heb. 13:5)

From that position of spiritual strength, your prayers cease being an exercise in trying to get God to do what you want. Rather, you find joy in praying (as Jesus taught us), "Your will be done, on earth as it is in heaven" (Matt. 6:10).

God uses trials to strip us of earthly desires and to put our confidence in Him alone. When you understand that, surviving the trials becomes secondary to learning to trust.

Today we have an advantage that Habakkuk lacked. We live on this side of the cross. We have a fuller revelation of the love of God and His care for His people. Look back to the love that caused Him to bear your sins in His body at Calvary.

> But God demonstrates His own love toward us, in that while we were yet sinners, Christ died for us.
> (Rom. 5:8)

How could you not trust in a God like that? When you remember Christ crucified, Christ resurrected, Christ ascended to glory, Christ interceding for you, Christ coming again—you can't help but be overwhelmed by the majesty, goodness, and faithfulness of God. It staggers our comprehension.

Can you submit to a God like that, even when you don't understand? Absolutely.

I realize that is a lofty spiritual challenge. In your present grief it may seem far away. But don't let that hinder you, my friend. The Lord is exposing these things to your mind so the Spirit of God can bring you to this place of sweet submission that Habakkuk knew.

The trust and subsequent joy you see in Habakkuk is not limited to a special prophet or specially favored Christians today. This is available to all of us in the worst of times. We can all live in this kind of spiritual victory when we know the God whose ways are above us all.

In 1758, Sarah Edwards heard the news that her husband, Jonathan Edwards, had died suddenly at the age of fifty-seven. America lost its greatest theologian and Sarah lost her life companion. Soon after, she wrote these words to her daughter, Esther, to express her reaction:

What shall I say? A holy and good God has covered us with a dark cloud. O that we may kiss the rod, and lay our hands on our mouths! The Lord has done it. He has made me adore his goodness, that we had him so long. But my God lives; and he has my heart. O what a legacy my husband, and your father, has left us! We are all given to God, and there I am, and love to be.[9]

Sarah Edwards yielded to God in her time of trial. That point of submission is the goal to which the Spirit is leading our hearts in our own times of adversity.

---

9 Quoted in Iain H. Murray, *Jonathan Edwards: A New Biography* (Edinburgh: The Banner of Truth Trust, 1988), 442.

11

God's Ways Have Been Proven in the Past

Habakkuk 3:3–15

. . . .

Beloved, do not be surprised at the fiery ordeal among you, which comes upon you for your testing, as though some strange thing were happening to you; but to the degree that you share the sufferings of Christ, keep on rejoicing, so that also at the revelation of His glory you may rejoice with exultation.
(1 Peter 4:12–13)

Trusting God is not a blind step of irrational faith. Rather, it is a volitional, heart response to an understanding of God's revealed truth. Habakkuk will show us this in 3:3–15. Judgment and a long exile lie just ahead. How did he not fall into immense discouragement?

In this section of his book, Habakkuk is remembering how God acted on behalf of His people in the past—prior to the rise of the Chaldeans, prior to Habakkuk's birth, indeed, several centuries into the past. He is rehearsing Israel's salvation history.

God had delivered them from slavery in Egypt under the leadership of Moses. He had given them supernatural victories in battle. Habakkuk remembers this history to provide a framework for strengthened faith that God would one day act again to deliver Israel.

Habakkuk 3:3–15 is an intricate passage filled with obscure geographic references and poetic language that makes it difficult to understand when you read through it for the first time. Before we look at the highlights, the key to understanding the passage is found in 3:13.

> You went forth for the salvation of Your people,
> For the salvation of Your anointed.
> You struck the head of the house of the evil
> To lay him open from thigh to neck. Selah.
> (Hab. 3:13)

His point of recollection is that God was faithful to deliver His people in their past adversity. He struck down their enemies so that Israel could live. That past deliverance strengthens hope for a future deliverance after the coming exile. We'll consider just two verses in the passage.

> Did the LORD rage against the rivers, or was Your anger against the rivers, or was Your wrath against the sea, that You rode on Your horses, on your chariots of salvation? (Hab. 3:8)

In verse 8, Habakkuk remembers several occasions on which God delivered His people:

- He turned the Nile River into blood (Ex. 7:20–21);
- He parted the Red Sea (Ex. 14:21–29);
- He parted the Jordan River (Josh. 3:14–17).

To focus on only one of these incidents, you remember how the Egyptian army had the nation pinned against the Red Sea. It looked like a slaughter was imminent. But God supernaturally parted the sea. Israel walked through on dry land. When the Egyptians followed, the sea returned to normal and swallowed them alive (Ex. 14).

Habakkuk asks rhetorically if God was angry with the sea at that time. Had He exercised His power against the water to punish the sea? The implied answer is obviously "no."

No, God divided the sea to save His people from harm. In their extreme and urgent distress, God supernaturally intervened to save them and destroy their enemies. That historical act serves to remind Habakkuk and his readers that God is omnipotent. He has complete power to preserve and protect His people.

Habakkuk also recalls when God made the sun and moon stand still.

Sun and moon stood in their places;
They went away at the light of Your arrows,
At the radiance of Your gleaming spear.
(Hab. 3:11)

He supernaturally extended the daylight so Joshua could complete his victory in battle (Josh. 10:12–14). God had again used His might to rescue His beleaguered people.

In full covenant love and faithfulness, God used His power on their behalf to deliver them from danger and into safety. He acted decisively to help them. That's what God does. He is strong to save His people in their hour of need.

Habakkuk and his contemporary audience needed these reminders as they anticipated a foreign invasion. Judgment was just ahead. They found encouragement to persevere through their collective memory of the great work of God in the past. It helped them understand what He would eventually do in the future.

In other words, Habakkuk isn't merely giving us a history lesson. He remembers the past *as a basis to understand what God will do in the future.* He piles up miraculous acts to prove that the future will eventually be bright.

Despite their sin, God had not abandoned His covenant people. Yes, He was bringing judgment, but it was a temporary time of correction that left the door open for long-term future blessing. The God who saved them in the past would be able and willing to rescue them again in coming days.

God had not changed since He led Israel out of Egypt, split the Red Sea, or made the sun stand still. He never changes. Surely, then, He would deliver His people in the future as He had in the past.

Today, we have the benefit of hindsight. God kept His promises. The Chaldeans did carry the Jews into exile, but it lasted only seventy years. The Chaldeans were later conquered by Persia in 539 BC. Soon thereafter, the Jews returned to their land. God revived the nation while it was in captivity. In so doing, he answered Habakkuk's prayer from 3:2:

Revive Your work in the midst of the years, in the midst of the years make it known; in wrath remember mercy. (Hab. 3:2)

The spiritual use of history is a critical component of trusting God in trying times. When adversity or disappointment strikes, you trust God by stepping back and considering what He has done in the past that would give you confidence that He will help you in what lies ahead.

As Christians, we have more to remember than Habakkuk did. Our great God is the One who became flesh in Jesus Christ and acted for our salvation on the cross. This great God bore our sins in His body. This great God is the One who rose from the dead when all seemed so hopeless as Jesus lay buried in the tomb. This great God is the One who ascended to heaven and sits at the right hand of the Majesty on High. This great God is coming again to take us to our eternal home (John 14:1–3).

Is that not enough to help you trust God? Think further. Look back on your own personal salvation. He chose you before the foundation of the world based on His grace. Then, He saved you at a particular point in your life and has been working in your life ever since. You've known His earthly blessings in the past. You look back and see how He worked out situations in ways you never could have dreamed at the moment.

He is the same God now that He was back then. So even though the circumstances have changed, God has not. Just as God blessed you in the past, so also He will bless you again in the future.

As you remember that history, your trials crumble in their power and importance before the greatness of God in history.

So you gather confidence for coming days as you remember God's ways from the past. God has done so much. We tend to forget how He once helped us. We need to call those things to mind and remind ourselves that if He was faithful then, He'll be faithful now.

Child of God, you have so many places to go to find encouragement for your soul. Look to the past and remember.

Behind you and in front of you. Above you and below you.

You are surrounded with the goodness, greatness, and grace of God. All those things are independent of your present circumstances.

Perhaps you are wiping tears off your cheeks as you read this, but you can say, "God, even in the midst of this, I trust You. I know this turns out with You displaying Your love and faithfulness to me. That's all I need to know."

You look back over biblical history. You consider the out-working of providence since the completion of the canon of Scripture. You consider God's grace in your own life.

And having meditated on all those wonders, you conclude from the past that He will bless you yet again. You may not see the fulfillment of His promise in this life, but it is assured.

And with the past settled in your mind, you can begin to trust God for the future in the midst of your trying times.

12

God's Ways Bring Transcendent Joy

Habakkuk 3:16–19

. . . .

Rejoice in the Lord always; again I will say, rejoice!
(Philippians 4:4)

By now, we have laid the foundation necessary to answer this question: Can a Christian be genuinely joyful in the midst of severe adversity which cannot change and might even get worse?

Yes. You can be content despite your circumstances. Christ is sufficient to satisfy your soul, no matter what else happens in life. The book of Habakkuk ends on precisely that note, even in the midst of the prophet being very human in the process.

> I heard and my inward parts trembled,
> At the sound my lips quivered.
> Decay enters my bones,
> And in my place I tremble.
> Because I must wait quietly for the day of distress,
> For the people to arise who will invade us.
> (Hab. 3:16)

Habakkuk begins with a description of the physical impact his dialogue with God has had upon him. He trembles because he must wait for the coming invasion of the Chaldeans. Even though Habakkuk has surrendered to the Lord's plan for this situation, the awfulness of what is to come still affects him deeply. Life as he and his people have known it would soon come to an end.

Habakkuk is transparent about his feelings and trembles at what he is about to experience. This physical reaction is not inconsistent with godliness. There is a difference between lacking faith and having weakness in the flesh.

True faith can live even when the flesh is weak. You see this in great men throughout the Bible. Remember Paul wrote in in 1 Corinthians 2:3 how "[he] was with you in weakness and in fear and in much trembling." It should comfort our hearts, especially as we remember the words of Psalm 103:14: "He Himself knows our frame; He is mindful that we are but dust."

I make that point because we all know Christians who give the air of always having everything under control, always having the answer to everything, and never having any problems. My answer to that is that Scripture knows of no such person. The psalmists continually cried to the Lord in time of need. Even our Lord said, "My soul is deeply grieved, to the point of death" (Matt. 26:38).

The invading army would soon be on the doorstep. What then?

Though the fig tree should not blossom
And there be no fruit on the vines,
Though the yield of the olive should fail
And the fields produce no food,
Though the flock should be cut off from the fold
And there be no cattle in the stalls,
Yet I will exult in the LORD,
I will rejoice in the God of my salvation.
(Hab. 3:17–18)

The devastation which he anticipated was broad and deep. The choicest products of the land as well as the necessities of life would not be available to the prophet or his people. Destruction and poverty would cover the land where milk and honey once had flowed.

He realistically assesses the fact that life as he has known it will soon come to an end. Bloodthirsty men are about to swoop down, and he can't do anything about it. He can't run. He can't hide. And it gives him the shivers.

And yet Habakkuk's soul is rejoicing. The theme is one of

exuberant singing and shouting. How can that be?

If you had been there, perhaps you would have spoken to him like this: "Habakkuk, this is tragic! You're going to be swept into exile! You're going to have brutal oppressors reigning over you—and you're joyful? Are you mad?"

No, Habakkuk isn't mad. He's a man of God. He understands true, rich, deep biblical joy that looks circumstances squarely in the face and says, "Yes, I admit it all. But that is secondary to something bigger in my life. It is more important to me that God is who He is than what my circumstances are. God is great and sovereign and good and faithful to His people no matter what happens to me in this life."

Habakkuk is showing you that biblical joy is completely independent of your circumstances. Nothing has to change for you to know this kind of fullness of joy. God's character *alone* gives the believing heart grounds for jubilation.

Despite the complete adversity of the circumstances, Habakkuk says, "I will exult in the Lord, I will rejoice in the God of my salvation." Taken together, these verbs speak of an enthusiastic, expressive rejoicing.

The nature of God alone gives Habakkuk ground for jubilation because God ultimately controls and directs the status of peoples and nations. Habakkuk is not only describing present rejoicing. He is expressing a commitment to rejoice in the future as well.

The faithful, loyal love of God is sufficient to bring joy to Habakkuk. There are no external circumstances whatsoever to prompt contentment. It's all gone. But Habakkuk is satisfied in life because he is satisfied with God.

> The Lord GOD is my strength,
> And He has made my feet like hinds' feet,
> And makes me walk on my high places.
> (Hab. 3:19)

It is the picture of a mountain sheep climbing up treacherous heights where it would be easy to fall. But he climbs with success and surefootedness. So in the same way you, as one of the Lord's people, can reach the heights of spiritual victory even in the midst of severe obstacles and setbacks. This is where God wants to take you.

Habakkuk says, in effect, "When I'm in this place of trusting God like I should, I can walk through this coming judgment with confidence. Just like a mountain sheep climbs steep places and is secure in the midst of the danger, so also I am safe in the midst of this calamity. I'll walk through this because of who my God is. I'll be on firm ground while I do."

He had shown the faithful Jews a pattern for how they should face coming judgment. In the process, God has also given us principles that we can follow to walk through adversity in our own lives.

The remarkable thing about this conclusion is that Habakkuk's circumstances had not changed. In fact, they were worse than he had realized, because he didn't know about the invasion before the book started. But his perspective had changed, and that made all the difference. He was no longer concerned about outward circumstances. He was satisfied simply to know his God. He had joy.

The genius of Habakkuk's message is that it reveals God's grand scheme of dealing with nations while simultaneously showing His kindness to a single soul. The God who moves in world history also comforts the human heart.

Joy is available to every believer in Christ in the worst trials he or she faces.

That does not mean that you are oblivious to your position or deny the reality of the problems you are about to face.

Trusting God does not mean that you do not feel your weakness. It does not mean that you never feel fear in the midst of an uncertain future. Those things are not inconsistent with faith.

Habakkuk teaches us not to deny obvious reality. He teaches us to rely on Christ and then know joy, nonetheless.

The remarkable aspect of Habakkuk's faith is that it is far more than a passive resignation to the inevitable. Though life crumbles around him, he will have joy in the sufficiency of God.

My friend, that is supernatural Christian living. This is the Christian man or woman who appraises life and says, "Yes, I see all the woe and misery. But that is secondary to something transcendent. I will exult in the Lord. I will rejoice in the God of my salvation."

The Christian life, truly glorifying God in the midst of your trials, is more than maintaining a stiff upper lip when trials come. It's more than *just* folding your arms across your chest and saying, "I'll be a rock." It's not about escaping your problems by getting busy with something else. It's more than biding time until things get better.

No, no, no—a thousand times, no! The glory of the Christian life is to face your problems and say, "It's all very grim from an earthly, human perspective. *But that is not the perspective that governs my heart!* I know the living God. He is good. He is in control. He has forgiven my sins through the Lord Jesus Christ. He has set His affection on me. Therefore, knowing these things, my heart will rest in supernatural joy because it is in union with a supernatural Christ who will never let me go. I belong to Christ. That's all I need."

Habakkuk had learned the critical lesson in spiritual life. He is in his circumstances, yet above them, when he trusts the living God. When you come to that position, your joy is unassailable. That assurance guards your heart like a fortress.

So, my friend, take these great truths about God and His ways . . . and rejoice. He is worthy of that kind of response from you. This world is not your home.

Habakkuk thus proves the reality of the phrase, "The just shall live by faith," which he had earlier penned in 2:4b. Faith was no barren theory to him. Faith was life itself.

In the same way, the apostle Paul wrote words in Romans 8 that make it clear:

> But in all these things we overwhelmingly conquer through Him who loved us. For I am convinced that

neither death, nor life, nor angels, nor principalities, nor things present, nor things to come, nor powers, nor height, nor depth, nor any other created thing, will be able to separate us from the love of God, which is in Christ Jesus our Lord.
(Rom. 8:37–39)

Herein lies the great encouragement of the book of Habakkuk to present-day believers. God patiently brought him to a place of deep trust as Habakkuk honestly wrestled with profound questions about the character and ways of God. God did not abandon him to his struggles.

Rather, God brought him through the discouragement to a position of remarkable trust, where disappointment with God had been banished. God changed Habakkuk, not the situation.

The experience of Habakkuk serves as an example to Christians today (*cf.* James 5:10). He dealt honestly with his questions before God when his experience did not seem to match what he intellectually knew to be true about God. Habakkuk persisted in faith even when the questions became increasingly difficult. In the process, he discovered more fully the sufficiency of God.

You can live with the same faith today, even if seemingly insurmountable difficulties intrude upon your walk with God. You can trust God even though all blessings fail. As trials cause you to plunge more deeply into the nature of His character and ways, you will one day find yourself with a richer, more profound experience of the God of your salvation.

The Lord is good, the Lord is in control, and He has set His affection on you. Christ died and rose again. That's all you really need. It doesn't make the problem go away, but it provides the means to overcome the struggle.

You can draw close to God even when the hardest times hit you. But the way forward is not longing for a change in circumstances. It's not believing that God will quickly change the situation. It is the very character of God Himself. Come what may, you can rejoice solely in the person and work of Christ and being in His hand (*cf.* John 10:28).

As your trials cause you to search more deeply into His character and ways, you will one day find yourself with a richer knowledge of Christ and with a deeper joy than you knew was even possible. You'll find that God has led you to a great triumph in Christ. You will be glad and give all the glory to Him.

May God bless that truth to the eternal good of your soul.

13

Epilogue

That is Enough
· · · · · · · · · · · · · · ·

*Beloved, now we are children of God, and it has not appeared as
yet what we will be. We know that when He appears, we will be
like Him, because we will see Him just as He is.*
(1 John 3:2)

I remember the precise moment when all of these principles about God's ways clicked together for me. I was writing a seminary paper on Habakkuk, several years after the plane crash. I had labored on it for weeks.

I was sitting at my desk and read again the words "I will exult in the LORD; I will rejoice in the God of my salvation." I involuntarily jumped out of my chair and said, "That's it!"

God, through His Word, had given me the answer that the pastor couldn't. It was so simple and yet so profound.

God is who He is.

That is enough.

I didn't need answers to my questions. I didn't need anything else. Everything—including the eternal state of my dear father's soul—was subordinate to the glory of God.

I didn't have to figure anything out. I didn't have to believe God for things He had not revealed. He is sovereign over the universe. Christ loved me and gave Himself up for me at the cross (Gal. 2:20).

That's all I need and all I need to know. My gracious Lord, having secured my soul, will secure everything else that pertains to me. The details do not matter. The final reality does.

An extended period of joy inexpressible and full of glory filled my soul after I finished that paper (*cf.* 1 Peter 1:8–9) that surpassed the depth of gloom I had known before. Christ had kept me through it all. He will keep me until I see Him face to face. What else matters in light of that?

Don't get the wrong impression. The intense emotions of

those days eventually faded as life went on. And after all these years, I still have to recite those principles from Habakkuk when new adversities strike. Sometimes I still act like a beginner in the school of faith.

At the end of the day, "We all stumble in many ways" (James 3:2).

But still. Scripture is sufficient to restore the soul (Ps. 19:7). Christ truly gives rest to the weary and heavy-laden (Matt. 11:28–30). The Word of God certifies these realities to the believing heart.

Christ gave rest to this unworthy sinner. He promises the same rest to you.

But that still leaves some hard questions. What about my dear dad? What about your unbelieving loved ones who have died, apparently without Christ?

Dear friend, we don't find our comfort in minimizing the warnings of Scripture about the final judgment of those who reject Christ. Nor do we run to a speculative hope that says, "Maybe he trusted Christ before he died." Maybe he did—but Christian joy must be based on truth, not speculation or wishful thinking.

Our hope is in God, not man. We must leave the eternal state of our departed loved ones in the hands of the Judge of all the earth to deal justly with their souls. Whatever He does will be right (*cf.* Gen. 18:25).

> As for God, His way is blameless; the word of the LORD is tried; He is a shield to all who take refuge in Him.
> (Ps. 18:30)

The following simple thought has given me much comfort over the years.

I have entrusted my soul to Christ. If I can trust Him with my soul, I can trust Him with the souls of all I have ever loved as well. I don't pronounce final judgment and neither do I indulge false hope.

Christ reigns. He is sovereign, holy, good, and wise. That is enough. We look up to Him in praise rather than look down to the grave in anxiety.

And one day, you and I will see Him in His resurrected glory, face-to-face. One glimpse of Him will ravish our hearts. We will know His supremacy. All our doubts and questions will be swallowed up in complete and irreversible victory.

> Beloved, now we are children of God, and it has not appeared as yet what we will be. We know that when He appears, we will be like Him, because we will see Him just as He is.
> (1 John 3:2)

Martyn Lloyd-Jones says:

> Do you know that you are destined to see Him as He is? Blessed, glorious vision to see the Son of God in all His glory, as He is, face to face—you standing and looking at Him and enjoying Him for all eternity. It is only then that we will begin to understand what He did for us, the price He paid, the cost of our salvation. Oh, let us hold on to this! Shame on us for ever grumbling; shame on us for ever saying that the Christian life is too hard; shame on us for ever half-heartedly worshipping, praising, and loving Christ and His glory. You and I are destined for that vision glorious; we shall see Him as He is, face to face.[10]

My friend, that is enough.

---

10 D. Martyn Lloyd-Jones, *Life in Christ: Studies in 1 John* (Wheaton, IL: Crossway Books, 2002), 291–92.

14

What If You Are Not a Christian?

Don't Waste Your Sorrow
. . . .

I tell you, no, but unless you repent, you will all likewise perish.
(Luke 13:5)

Up to this point, I've been writing to those who are true Christians. In this chapter, I want to say a word to those who know they are not Christians, or at least have serious questions about their salvation.

What does *your* suffering mean in the purposes of God? God has stopped your world. Why would he do that? Only Scripture can give you clarity and direction.

> Now on the same occasion there were some present who reported to Him about the Galileans whose blood Pilate had mixed with their sacrifices. And Jesus said to them, "Do you suppose that these Galileans were greater sinners than all other Galileans because they suffered this fate? I tell you, no, but unless you repent, you will all likewise perish. Or do you suppose that those eighteen on whom the tower in Siloam fell and killed them were worse culprits than all the men who live in Jerusalem? I tell you, no, but unless you repent, you will all likewise perish." (Luke 13:1–5)

In that text, Jesus addresses two contemporary events that were the subject of much public discussion in his day. The Roman governor, Pilate, had killed certain worshippers at the temple. Separately, eighteen people died in a tower collapse.

People wanted to speculate why disaster had fallen on the dead. Did God single out those deceased victims because they were so sinful?

Jesus did not accept the way the question was framed. He pivoted from the dead to the living to make a single point:

Unless you repent, you will all likewise perish.

Christ challenged their false sense of security as they abstractly speculated on spiritual matters. He also rebuked their spiritual pride. Yes, Jesus' hearers had been spared that particular calamity.

But they would face eternal judgment if they themselves did not repent. The nineteenth-century writer J.C. Ryle says:

> [Jesus took] the opportunity to speak to them about their own souls. He told them to look within themselves and think about their own standing before God. What if these Galileans did die a sudden death? What is that to you? Consider your own ways. Unless you repent, you will perish in the same way.[11]

Christ used the occasion to call His hearers to turn from their wicked, godless ways and to turn to God with a faith that was willing to obey Him. The message is the same today.

My friend, perhaps you're reading this book and your own world has collapsed—even suddenly, like mine did.

Have you lost your job or your health? Has a financial reversal left you without the security you had planned? Has your family life hurt you deeply in ways that make life miserable?

Perhaps worse, do you feel the regret of past decisions that you now see were foolish and brought painful consequences that you cannot change?

Before we go any further, let me give you two immediate assurances of hope. Scripture can help you. God can still be gracious to you. For that to happen, you need to listen to His Word and consider things beyond your earthly problem.

We can start with this simple observation: your adversity is

11   J.C. Ryle, *Luke*, The Crossway Classic Commentaries, series eds. Alister McGrath and J. I. Packer (Wheaton, IL: Crossway Books, 1997) 183.

teaching you that you are not in control of your life. Setbacks occur to the young, the wealthy, and the privileged—as well as to the rest of us. *None* of us is exempt from trouble.

What do these trials mean? How can you benefit from them?

1.Remember God's Hand

The first thing you need to do is look beyond the so-called natural causes of your trouble. What you see, by itself, does not explain your sorrow. There is an unseen purpose at work that you must consider. Ephesians 1:11 says:

> [We have been] predestined according to His purpose who works all things after the counsel of His will.

That's a really important statement. God has planned and directs everything that happens. That includes what has happened, or is happening, in your personal life. Jesus said:

> Are not two sparrows sold for a cent? And yet not one of them will fall to the ground apart from your Father. But the very hairs of your head are all numbered. (Matt. 10:29–30)

The God of the Bible is at work in everything that happens—the big things and the seemingly small things. The nineteenth-century pastor Charles Spurgeon said:

> We believe that God sends all pestilences, let them come how they may. He sends them with a purpose. We conceive that it is our business as ministers of God, to call the people's attention to God in the disease, and teach them the lesson God would have them learn.[12]

12   Charles Haddon Spurgeon, "The Voice of the Cholera," A Sermon Preached on August 12, 1866. https://www.spurgeon.org/resource-library/sermons/the-voice-of-the-cholera

What is the lesson God would have *you* learn? Stay with me.

2. Remember God's Holiness

God is not like us. He is morally pure. He is separate from evil.

> Your eyes are too pure to approve evil, and You cannot look on wickedness with favor.
> (Hab. 1:13)

The holiness of God—whose hand is in all things—matters. Consider the prophet Isaiah.

> In the year of King Uzziah's death I saw the Lord sitting on a throne, lofty and exalted, with the train of His robe filling the temple. Seraphim stood above Him, each having six wings: with two he covered his face, and with two he covered his feet, and with two he flew. And one called out to another and said,
> "Holy, Holy, Holy, is the LORD of hosts, the whole earth is full of His glory."
> And the foundations of the thresholds trembled at the voice of him who called out, while the temple was filling with smoke. Then I said,
> "Woe is me, for I am ruined! Because I am a man of unclean lips, and I live among a people of unclean lips; for my eyes have seen the King, the LORD of hosts."
> (Isaiah 6:1–5).

The prophet was undone in God's presence. God is so holy and righteous that no one escapes from His searching view.

> And there is no creature hidden from His sight, but all things are open and laid bare to the eyes of Him with whom we have to do.
> (Heb. 4:13)

Dear reader, if I am to help you, I must ask you to consider this question. What does a holy God see when He looks on your life?

- Does He see someone marked by the fear of God?
- Does He see someone who heeds His Word?
- Does He see someone repenting of sin?
- Or does He perhaps see someone who has pursued other interests in life, but not the Lord Jesus Christ?

Does He see someone who has easily taken His name in vain and has had no desire to worship Him or honor His authority? Spurgeon further comments:

> The masses of our people regard not God, care not for the Lord Jesus, and have no thought about eternal things. This is a Christian [nation] we sometimes say, but where shall be found more thorough heathens than we find here?[13]

That leads us into the most difficult thing of all to contemplate.

3. Remember God's Hell

Friend, your adversity should cause you to consider the state of your soul. That was Jesus' whole point in Luke 13. Consider these other Scriptures as well:

> For You are not a God who takes pleasure in wickedness; no evil dwells with You. The boastful shall not stand before Your eyes; you hate all who do iniquity. You destroy those who speak falsehood; the LORD abhors the man of bloodshed and deceit.
> (Ps. 5:4–6)

13   Spurgeon, "The Voice of the Cholera"

For the wrath of God is revealed from heaven against all ungodliness and unrighteousness of men who suppress the truth in unrighteousness, because that which is known about God is evident within them; for God made it evident to them. For since the creation of the world His invisible attributes, His eternal power and divine nature, have been clearly seen, being understood through what has been made, so that they are without excuse. For even though they knew God, they did not honor Him as God or give thanks, but they became futile in their speculations, and their foolish heart was darkened.
(Rom. 1:18–21)

God's present wrath will yield to a greater eternal wrath.

Then I saw a great white throne and Him who sat upon it, from whose presence earth and heaven fled away, and no place was found for them. And I saw the dead, the great and the small, standing before the throne, and books were opened; and another book was opened, which is the book of life; and the dead were judged from the things which were written in the books, according to their deeds. And the sea gave up the dead which were in it, and death and Hades gave up the dead which were in them; and they were judged, every one of them according to their deeds. Then death and Hades were thrown into the lake of fire. This is the second death, the lake of fire. And if anyone's name was not found written in the book of life, he was thrown into the lake of fire.
(Rev. 20:11–15)

In His great holiness, God will judge unsaved people forever in a lake of fire.

My friend, what will happen to you at that terrible time?

Who will help you *then* if you are not in control *now*?

You see, God has brought earthly trouble to you so that you will think about an even greater eternal trouble.

He wants you to consider the state of your soul, while there is still time to do something about it.

4. Remember God's Hope

So what are you to do? There is only one place for you to go. God will meet you at the cross of Jesus Christ.

It was at the cross where Jesus did a reconciling work for sinners. He shed His blood to cover the sins of people like you.

Your trials may *look* like an act of judgment. But my friend, it's something much different. It is actually a display of *grace*.

Yes, grace.

God sends us adversity so that we might see in an undeniable way our weakness. He does that so that we might turn to Him for safety and salvation.

You must see the purpose of God in your time of crisis. Again, Charles Spurgeon gives perspective in a time of trial that affected many in his nation:

> If you ask me what I think to be the design, I believe it to be this—to wake up our indifferent population, to make them remember that there is a God, to render them susceptible to the influences of the gospel, to drive them to the house of prayer, [and] to influence their minds to receive the Word.[14]

God sent this crisis in grace to awaken you from spiritual slumber. He sent it so you might be rescued from eternal death. Will you respond to Him? He has sent you advance warning. For a brief time longer, He extends His hand in mercy.

> For God so loved the world, that He gave His only begotten Son, that whoever believes in Him shall not perish, but have eternal life.
> (John 3:16)

14 Spurgeon, "The Voice of the Cholera"

Christ will help you. He shed His blood on the cross of Calvary to wash away the sins of all who call upon Him.

> Therefore many other signs Jesus also performed in the presence of the disciples, which are not written in this book; but these have been written so that you may believe that Jesus is the Christ, the Son of God; and that believing you may have life in His name.
> (John 20:30–31)

> He made Him who knew no sin to be sin on our behalf, so that we might become the righteousness of God in Him.
> (2 Cor. 5:21)

> For Christ also died for sins once for all, the just for the unjust, so that He might bring us to God.
> (1 Peter 3:18)

May the Spirit help you turn to Christ while He is near.

> The Spirit and the bride say, "Come." And let the one who hears say, "Come." And let the one who is thirsty come; let the one who wishes take the water of life without cost.
> (Rev. 22:17)

Christ graciously calls you to receive the free gift of salvation by faith alone. He will receive you, forgive you, and give you new hope and purpose in life. I would love nothing more than for that work of God to take place in your heart.

That is the purpose which God intends in your trials. It is a good and gracious purpose. But my friend, be warned:

Unless you repent, you will all likewise perish.

THE TRUTH PULPIT

Teaching God's People God's Word

To learn more about Don Green and his Bible-teaching resources, visit thetruthpulpit.com. You can subscribe to podcasts of his full-length messages from Truth Community Church, the daily "The Truth Pulpit" radio program, and his weekly feature "Through the Psalms."

Also by Don Green

John MacArthur began his ministry at Grace Community Church in Sun Valley, California in 1969. Since then, millions have known him as a steadfast voice for biblical authority and teaching. But what kind of man is he in private? Don Green observed him closely over a fifteen-year period in leadership roles at Grace Church and Grace to You. *In John MacArthur: An Insider's Tribute*, you'll find winsome vignettes, exclusive interviews, and never-before-published photos to give you access to the man whose service to Christ has benefitted so many—all as a testimony to the grace of God in the life of John MacArthur.

John MacArthur: An Insider's Tribute
Deluxe Coffee-Table Quality Hardback, Color Throughout, 80pp
ISBN 978–0–9987156–0–5
www.ttwpress.com

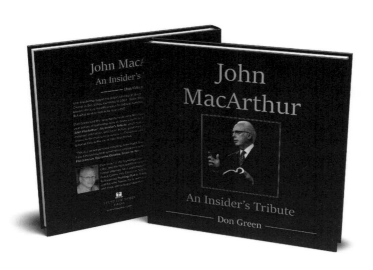

Also by Don Green

New Book Coming Soon

"Lord, to whom shall we go?
You have the words of eternal life."
(John 6:68)

With those words, the apostle Peter recognized the eternal and irreplaceable value of the words that fell from the lips of the Lord Jesus Christ. But does the same reverence animate the ivory towers of New Testament scholarship?

In this forthcoming book, Don Green takes you behind the scenes to warn you about a troubling trend that erodes confidence in Scripture. He defends the reliability of the Gospels—those inspired writings given to man so that we may believe that Jesus is the Christ, the Son of God, and that by believing we may have life in His name.

Did Jesus Really Say?
New Testament Scholarship and the Integrity of the Gospels

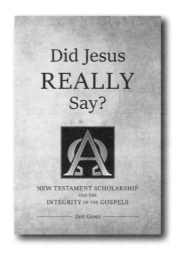